COOKING WITH

Bon Appétit

COOKING WITH
Bon Appétit

Recipe
Yearbook
1993

Editors' Choice of Recipes from 1992

THE KNAPP PRESS
Publishers
Los Angeles

Library of Congress Catalog Number: 92-075808

ISBN: 0-89535-997-9

On the Cover: *Triple Berry Tart*
Photographed by David Bishop.

Printed and bound in the United States of America
10   9   8   7   6   5   4   3   2   1

🍎 Contents

❧ Foreword

Remember your high-school yearbook, the way it managed to sum up an entire year in photographs—candid ones snapped here and there, posed portraits and group shots? Well, this is *Bon Appétit*'s version of the high-school yearbook, only ours tells the year's story in recipes—more than 175 of them to be exact—and words. This is our seventh annual yearbook, and it's filled with our very favorite recipes, culled from the many hundreds we featured over the course of 1992, and select reviews of the year's hottest products, places and people.

The recipes here are chosen by those most in the know—the magazine's editors. Some of the recipes are intended to represent the most interesting trends of the past year (low-fat cooking, for example), others are just flat out favorites—dishes remembered for their unique combination of ingredients, their inspired technique or their irresistible taste. They cover all the bases, from appetizers through desserts, from down-home simple to restaurant-style sophisticated. There are dishes for quick family suppers and others for elegant late-night dinner parties, for big casual get-togethers and romantic meals *à deux*. In other words, whatever the occasion, it's likely you'll find the ideal recipe in these pages.

In addition to all kinds of recipes, you'll find all types of recipes. Virtually every corner of the world is represented here in dishes that look and taste exotic without being difficult to prepare or calling for impossible-to-find ingredients. Every chapter mixes and matches international inspirations: In "Main Courses," for example, Moroccan-Style Cornish Game Hens and Chicken-stuffed Bell Peppers Spanish Style make appearances alongside Chinese Smoked Chicken, Hot and Spicy Pork Vindaloo and Grilled Leg of Lamb with Chimichurri Sauce.

And we didn't stop at recipes for every occasion from every popular cuisine: There are also dishes here for all kinds of diets—whether you're trying to cut back on salt, reduce your fat intake, watch your cholesterol or simply count calories—because eating healthy is something many of us have really taken to heart over this past and previous years. Look up

Roast Pheasant with Apples, Stir-fried Rice with Vegetables, Garlic-Lime Chicken and Vegetable Paella to see what we mean.

What would any yearbook be without a look back at the people and trends that helped shape the course of the year? You'll find ours in the section called "News '92—The Year of Food and Entertaining in Review." It includes some of the year's best new products, foods you can order by mail, terrific books, hot chefs and happening restaurants, trendy getaways, new kitchen products—everything you need to know to keep you in the know. (All the prices, addresses and other details have been updated as of this book's publication date.)

You'll also note that we've left a couple of pages blank at the front and back of the book for—what else—signatures. Why not throw a party with a selection of terrific dishes from the upcoming pages and pass around your book for everyone to sign? You'll have a wonderful treasure to remember 1992 by.

1 ❦ Appetizers

Appetizers have a lot going for them: They stave off hunger; they awaken appetites with the promise of good things to come; they give the cook the gift of time, an extra few minutes in the kitchen to put the finishing touches on a meal; and they imply an opportunity to talk and drink and eat in a relaxed setting. Whatever the occasion, from a casual get-together for friends to an elaborate, celebratory dinner party, the appetizer you choose will set the tone for the meal and start things off on exactly the right note.

If you're planning a summertime barbecue for a crowd, consider the Crudités and Grilled Sausages with Sweet and Hot Chutneys—a platterful of colorful vegetables, sausage bites and bowls of chutney, one sweet and creamy, the other tangy and spicy. The cocktail party, popular again now, is the perfect occasion for the Pesto Cheesecake, a lovely, layered cake flavored with different cheeses, pesto and pine nuts, and served with crackers. For a Mexican-themed meal, get things going with Four-Pepper Salsa with Chips, which can be made a full two days ahead. And if you're in the mood for "dip" but want to be different, try the rich-tasting Kippered Salmon Dip with bagel chips.

Crudités and Grilled Sausages with Sweet and Hot Chutneys

12 servings

Vegetables to dip (such as carrot sticks, steamed broccoli florets, jicama and cauliflower)

3 pounds fully cooked sausages (such as bratwurst and kielbasa)
Sweet Chutney (see recipe)
Hot Chutney (see recipe)

Arrange vegetables around edge of platter. Grill or panfry sausages until brown and heated through. Cut into 1-inch pieces. Arrange sausage pieces in center of platter, placing toothpick in each piece. Serve with chutneys.

Sweet Chutney

Makes about 1½ cups

1 cup mayonnaise or reduced-calorie mayonnaise
⅔ cup Major Grey's Chutney

1 teaspoon curry powder
¼ teaspoon cayenne pepper

Blend all ingredients in processor. Transfer to bowl. (*Can be prepared 2 days ahead. Cover and refrigerate.*)

Hot Chutney

Makes about 2 cups

2 cups (packed) fresh mint leaves
2 cups (packed) fresh cilantro leaves
⅔ cup cider vinegar
¼ cup sugar
4 jalapeño chilies, seeded

1 2-inch fresh ginger piece, peeled, cut into ½-inch pieces
1 teaspoon salt
½ cup plain yogurt

Combine all ingredients except yogurt in processor and blend until very finely chopped. Mix in yogurt. Transfer chutney to bowl. (*Can be prepared 1 day ahead. Cover with plastic and refrigerate.*)

Shellfish with Spicy Island Dip

4 servings

1 cup canned crushed tomatoes with added puree
½ cup chopped onion
⅓ cup chopped pimiento-stuffed green olives

2 jalapeño chilies, seeded but not deveined, minced
1½ teaspoons cider vinegar

12 snow crab claws or cooked jumbo shrimp, shelled, deveined

Combine first 5 ingredients in medium bowl. Cover and refrigerate. (*Can be prepared 2 days ahead. Keep refrigerated.*)
Serve crab claws or shrimp with dipping sauce.

Pesto Cheesecake

18 servings

1 tablespoon butter, room temperature
¼ cup fine dry breadcrumbs
½ cup plus 2 tablespoons grated Parmesan cheese

2 8-ounce packages cream cheese, room temperature
1 cup ricotta cheese

¼ teaspoon salt
⅛ teaspoon cayenne pepper
3 large eggs
½ cup purchased pesto sauce
¼ cup pine nuts

Fresh basil sprigs
Crackers

Preheat oven to 325°F. Rub 1 tablespoon butter over bottom and sides of 9-inch-diameter springform pan. Mix breadcrumbs with 2 tablespoons grated cheese. Coat pan with crumb mixture.

Using electric mixer, beat cream cheese, ricotta, remaining ½ cup Parmesan, salt and cayenne in large bowl until light. Add eggs 1 at a time, beating well after each addition. Transfer half of mixture to medium bowl. Mix pesto into remaining half. Pour pesto mixture into prepared pan; smooth top. Carefully spoon plain mixture over; gently smooth top. Sprinkle with pine nuts. Bake cake until center no longer moves when pan is shaken, about 45 minutes. Transfer to rack and cool completely. Cover with plastic; chill overnight.

Run small sharp knife around pan sides to loosen cheesecake, if necessary. Release pan sides from cheesecake. Transfer cheesecake to platter. Garnish with fresh basil sprigs. Surround with crackers and serve.

Spicy Beef Empanadas

Makes about 20

1 tablespoon olive oil
½ pound lean ground beef
½ green bell pepper, chopped
2 tablespoons chopped garlic
⅓ cup raisins, chopped
¼ cup chopped pimiento-stuffed green olives
1½ tablespoons red wine vinegar
1 tablespoon all purpose flour

1¾ teaspoons ground allspice
1 teaspoon ground cumin
¼ teaspoon cayenne pepper
1 cup packed grated Monterey Jack cheese (about 4 ounces)
⅓ cup chopped fresh cilantro

2 12-ounce packages Big Country buttermilk refrigerator biscuits
2 egg yolks, beaten to blend (glaze)

Heat oil in heavy medium skillet over medium heat. Add beef, bell pepper and garlic. Cook until beef loses its pink color and vegetables begin to soften, breaking up beef with fork, about 6 minutes. Add raisins and next 6 ingredients and cook until mixture is thick, about 5 minutes. Season with salt and pepper. Mix cheese and cilantro into filling. (*Can be made 1 day ahead. Cover and chill.*)

Preheat oven to 375°F. Roll out 1 biscuit on lightly floured surface to 4-inch circle. Brush half of dough edge with glaze. Place 1 rounded tablespoon filling on dough. Fold dough over to create half circle; press edges to seal. Using fork tines, crimp edge decoratively. Place empanada on heavy large baking sheet. Brush with glaze. Repeat with remaining biscuits, filling and glaze.

Bake empanadas until golden brown, about 12 minutes. Serve.

Pork Saté with Peanut Dipping Sauce

6 servings

⅓ cup plus 1 tablespoon minced fresh lemongrass (from bottom 6 inches of stalk)
3 tablespoons fresh lime juice
2 tablespoons dark brown sugar
1 tablespoon soy sauce
2 garlic cloves, minced
¾ pound pork tenderloin, trimmed, cut into 3-inch-long, ½-inch-wide, ¼-inch-thick slices

1 cup (or more) canned low-salt chicken broth
½ cup creamy peanut butter (do not use old-fashioned style or freshly ground)
½ cup chopped onion
1 tablespoon coriander seeds
½ jalapeño chili, minced

12 8-inch bamboo skewers, soaked in water 30 minutes
Minced green onion tops

Mix 1 tablespoon lemongrass, 1 tablespoon lime juice, 1 tablespoon sugar, soy sauce and garlic in large bowl. Add pork; toss to coat with marinade. Let stand at least 30 minutes and up to 1 hour.

Meanwhile, mix remaining ⅓ cup lemongrass, remaining 2 tablespoons lime juice, remaining 1 tablespoon sugar, 1 cup broth, peanut butter, onion, coriander and jalapeño in heavy medium saucepan. Bring to boil, whisking frequently. Transfer mixture to blender and puree. Strain into heavy small saucepan, pressing on solids with back of spoon; discard solids. Simmer until reduced to thick sauce consistency, stirring frequently, about 6 minutes. (*Can be prepared 1 day ahead. Cover and refrigerate. Reheat before using, thinning with more chicken broth if necessary.*)

Preheat broiler. Thread 3 pork strips on each skewer. Broil until cooked through, about 3 minutes per side. Pour sauce into bowl; set in center of platter. Sprinkle with green onion. Surround with pork skewers and serve.

Goat Cheese and Sausage Crostini

Makes about 36

1½ pounds sweet Italian sausages
8 ounces soft fresh goat cheese (such as Montrachet)
¼ cup olive oil
4 garlic cloves, pressed
½ teaspoon dried thyme, crumbled

2 3-inch-wide 8-ounce sourdough bread flutes, sliced
Olive oil
⅔ cup drained oil-packed sun-dried tomatoes, sliced
¾ cup Kalamata olives,* halved, pitted
Fresh basil leaves

Cook sausages in heavy medium skillet over medium heat until cooked through, about 12 minutes. Cool. Cut diagonally into ¼-inch-thick slices.

Mix goat cheese, ¼ cup oil, garlic and thyme in small bowl. (*Can be prepared 8 hours ahead. Refrigerate sausages and cheese mixture separately.*)

Preheat oven to 400°F. Arrange bread on baking sheet. Brush with oil. Bake until lightly toasted, about 10 minutes. Cool slightly. Spread with goat cheese. Top with sausages, then tomatoes. Bake until heated through, about 5 minutes. Garnish with olives and basil.

*Black, brine-cured olives, available at Greek and Italian markets and some supermarkets.

Four-Pepper Salsa with Chips

Makes about 3½ cups

1 14½-ounce can Italian plum tomatoes, drained
1 medium onion, thinly sliced
½ cup coarsely chopped celery
1 4-ounce can diced green chilies, drained
⅓ cup chopped red bell pepper
⅓ cup chopped yellow bell pepper
⅓ cup chopped green bell pepper

¼ cup olive oil
2 tablespoons red wine vinegar
1 teaspoon mustard seeds
1 teaspoon ground coriander
1 teaspoon salt
1 teaspoon pepper
¼ cup chopped fresh cilantro
  Tortilla chips

Combine first 13 ingredients in processor. Finely chop using on/off turns. Transfer to bowl. Cover and chill at least 4 hours. (*Can be made 2 days ahead.*) Mix cilantro into salsa. Serve with chips.

Quesadillas with Brie, Mango and Chilies

The star ingredients in this appetizer may be an unusual trio, but their flavors come together beautifully. These can be done on the grill or in the broiler.

4 servings

1 poblano chili*
1 red bell pepper
½ cup water
1 medium onion, thinly sliced
2 tablespoons (¼ stick) butter, melted
2 tablespoons vegetable oil

1 ripe mango, peeled, pitted, chopped
2 tablespoons chopped fresh cilantro
8 ounces chilled Brie cheese, rind trimmed, cut into ¼-inch-wide strips
4 8-inch flour tortillas

Char chili and bell pepper over gas flame or in broiler until blackened on all sides. Wrap in paper bag and let stand 10 minutes to steam. Peel, core and seed. Rinse if necessary; pat dry and chop. Place in small bowl.

Bring ½ cup water to boil in heavy small saucepan. Add onion. Cover and remove from heat. Let stand until onion is wilted, about 10 minutes. Drain. Add onion to chili mixture. (*Can be prepared 1 day ahead. Cover and refrigerate.*)

Prepare barbecue (medium heat) or preheat broiler. Blend melted butter and vegetable oil in small bowl. Add chopped mango and chopped fresh cilantro to chili mixture. Place ¼ of Brie cheese strips on half of each flour tortilla. Top each with ¼ of chili-mango mixture. Season with salt and pepper. Fold over empty half of flour tortillas to enclose filling. Brush with butter mixture. Place quesadillas buttered side down on grill. Cook 30 seconds, turn 90 degrees and grill quesadillas 30 seconds. Butter uncooked side and turn over. Grill until cheese begins to melt, about 30 seconds. Cut each quesadilla into 3 pieces. Arrange quesadillas on platter and serve.

*A *poblano* is a fresh green chili, sometimes called a fresh *pasilla,* available at Latin American markets and also at some supermarkets.

Kippered Salmon Dip

12 servings

2 pounds kippered salmon* or other heavily smoked salmon
2 cups mayonnaise
¼ cup minced fresh dill
2 tablespoons chopped drained capers
2 teaspoons fresh lemon juice

Capers, lemon slices and fresh dill sprigs
Bagel chips or other crackers

Remove skin and bones from salmon. Place salmon in bowl and flake. Add mayonnaise and mix well. Mix in minced dill, chopped capers and fresh lemon juice. Season with pepper. Refrigerate at least 1 hour. (*Can be prepared 2 days ahead. Keep refrigerated.*)

Spoon salmon mixture into bowl. Garnish with capers, lemon and dill. Surround with bagel chips and serve.

*Also known as barbecued salmon and available packaged in the deli section of most supermarkets.

Cheese and Spinach Turnovers

Makes 12

1 tablespoon olive oil
½ cup diced red onion
2 garlic cloves, minced
2 fresh spinach bunches, stemmed, chopped
2 ounces soft fresh goat cheese (such as Montrachet)
⅓ cup toasted pine nuts
3 tablespoons grated Parmesan cheese

½ teaspoon minced fresh rosemary or ¼ teaspoon dried, crumbled
½ teaspoon grated lemon peel

4 frozen phyllo pastry sheets, thawed
½ cup (1 stick) unsalted butter, melted

Heat oil in heavy large skillet over medium heat. Add onion and garlic and sauté 5 minutes. Increase heat to high. Add spinach and sauté until wilted, about 5 minutes. Drain spinach mixture, pressing on solids to release as much liquid as possible. Transfer to bowl and cool completely. Add goat cheese, pine nuts, Parmesan, rosemary and lemon peel. Season to taste with salt and pepper. (*Can be made 1 day ahead; refrigerate.*)

Place 1 phyllo sheet on work surface. Cut lengthwise into 3 strips. Brush with butter. Place 1 rounded tablespoon filling at 1 end of dough strip. Starting at 1 corner, fold pastry over filling, forming triangle. Repeat, folding up length of pastry as for flag. Brush with butter. Repeat with remaining pastry, butter and filling. Transfer turnovers to baking sheet. (*Can be prepared 1 day ahead. Cover and chill.*) Preheat oven to 375°F. Bake turnovers until golden, about 12 minutes. Cool slightly and serve.

Liptauer Spread

This delicious Hungarian spread, known by its German name, is traditionally made with a soft, white ewe's-milk Liptó cheese for which cottage cheese has become the standard American replacement. Onions, paprika and caraway are the essential seasonings, but others can be added according to individual taste. Serve with fresh radishes, green onions and slices of pumpernickel bread for a colorful presentation.

6 servings

1 cup cottage cheese
¼ cup (½ stick) unsalted butter, room temperature
2 teaspoons paprika (preferably sweet Hungarian)
1½ teaspoons caraway seeds, crushed in mortar with pestle
¾ teaspoon dry mustard

3 tablespoons minced onion
2 tablespoons chopped cornichons*

Cocktail pumpernickel bread
Radishes with leaves attached
Green onions, trimmed

Blend cottage cheese and butter in processor until smooth. Blend in paprika, caraway and mustard. Transfer to small bowl. Mix in onion and cornichons. Transfer to crock. Cover and refrigerate at least 3 hours. (*Can be prepared up to 2 days ahead. Keep refrigerated.*)

Place crock of cheese in center of platter. Surround with bread. Serve with radishes and green onions.

*Tiny, brine-packed French pickles available at specialty foods stores and some supermarkets.

Goat Cheese with Olives and Sun-dried Tomatoes

6 servings

1 8-ounce jar oil-packed sun-dried tomatoes (do not drain)
2 large garlic cloves, halved
⅔ cup chopped pitted Kalamata olives*

12 ounces soft fresh goat cheese (such as Montrachet), sliced
French bread baguette slices
Fresh basil sprigs
Kalamata olives*

Combine tomatoes (with oil) and garlic in processor. Blend until as smooth as possible, stopping occasionally to scrape down sides of bowl. Transfer mixture to bowl. Mix in chopped olives (*Can be made 2 days ahead. Cover and chill. Bring to room temperature before continuing.*)

Place tomato mixture in center of platter. Surround with cheese and bread. Garnish with basil and olives.

*Black, brine-cured olives, available at Greek and Italian markets and some supermarkets.

Guacamole Auténtico

This recipe for the Mexican condiment can be increased easily to accommodate large groups. Serve it with chips or as part of a south-western buffet.

Makes about 1½ cups

1 large ripe avocado, peeled, pitted
1 small garlic clove, minced
⅓ cup purchased salsa, drained

Using fork, mash all ingredients together in small bowl. Season guacamole to taste with salt and pepper. Serve immediately.

2 ❦ *Soups and Salads*

If you're like a lot of people, soups and salads make appearances in many of the meals you prepare—as first courses and main dishes in the case of soups, as first courses, side dishes and entreés in the case of salads. Both are so versatile, they turn up time and again, season in and season out.

On a cold winter's night, there are few suppers more warming than a big bowl of steaming soup: Try the classic French Onion Soup here, topped with slices of toasted French bread and melted Gruyère cheese, or the rustic Italian Vegetable Soup, packed with all that's good for you. For a sophisticated start to an elegant dinner party, there's chilled Fresh Tomato-Corn Soup or indulgently rich Cream of Garlic Soup. If it's a simple soup-and-sandwich dinner you have in mind, make a batch of Quick Black Bean Soup to go with your favorite sandwich.

If we're interpreting current nutritional news correctly, it's almost as if you can't eat too many salads. There are plenty of good-for-you candidates here, including Cabbage, Snow Pea and Carrot Slaw, made with a spiced vinegar and oil dressing, and Bulgur Salad with Oriental Dressing, a refreshing way to "get your grains." For a light meal, a main-course salad can't be beat. Take a look at Wild Rice and Chicken Salad with Tarragon, and Shrimp, Orange and Olive Salad with Sherry Vinaigrette, both quick and easy to make. All you need add is a basket of bread.

❦ Soups

French Onion Soup

6 servings

2 tablespoons (¼ stick) unsalted butter
¼ cup vegetable oil
3½ pounds onions, thinly sliced
2 cups dry white wine
6 cups chicken stock or canned low-salt broth

12 ½-inch-thick French bread baguette slices, toasted
1 cup grated Gruyère cheese (about 4 ounces)

Melt butter with oil in heavy large pot over medium heat. Add onions, cover and cook until lightly colored, stirring occasionally, about 45 minutes. Add wine and bring to boil, scraping up any browned bits. Cook 5 minutes. Add stock and bring to simmer. Simmer uncovered 1½ hours. Season to taste with salt and pepper. (*Can be prepared 1 day ahead. Cover and refrigerate. Bring to simmer before continuing with recipe.*)

Preheat broiler. Ladle soup into broilerproof bowls. Top with slices of toasted French bread. Sprinkle with grated Gruyère cheese. Broil until cheese melts. Serve onion soup immediately.

Tortilla Soup

4 servings

1½ pounds large tomatoes, quartered
1 medium onion, quartered
½ cup plus 3 tablespoons vegetable oil
4 corn tortillas, coarsely chopped
6 garlic cloves, finely chopped
8 cups chicken stock or canned low-salt broth
¼ cup tomato paste
1 tablespoon chopped fresh cilantro
1 tablespoon ground cumin

2 teaspoons chili powder
2 bay leaves

3 corn tortillas, cut into 2-inch-long ¼-inch-wide strips

1 cup diced cooked chicken
1 avocado, peeled, pitted, diced
1 cup shredded cheddar cheese
Sour cream

Puree tomatoes and onion in processor until mixture is as smooth as possible. Heat 3 tablespoons vegetable oil in heavy large saucepan over medium heat. Add chopped tortillas and garlic and sauté 2 minutes. Add tomato-onion puree, chicken stock, tomato paste, cilantro, cumin, chili powder and bay leaves and bring to boil. Reduce heat and simmer 30 minutes. Season to taste with salt. Strain soup through coarse sieve, pressing on solids with back of spoon. (*Can be prepared 1 day ahead. Cover and refrigerate.*)

Heat remaining ½ cup vegetable oil in heavy large skillet over high heat. Add tortilla strips and cook until crisp and golden, about 3 minutes. Transfer to paper towels and drain well.

Bring soup to simmer. Ladle into bowls. Serve, passing tortilla strips, chicken, avocado, cheese and sour cream.

Seafood Chowder

2 to 4 servings

2 tablespoons olive oil
1 onion, sliced
1 celery stalk, chopped
2 garlic cloves, chopped
1 6½-ounce can chopped clams
1 10¾-ounce can tomato soup
1 8-ounce bottle clam juice
1 tablespoon tomato paste

1 pound red snapper fillets, cut
   into 1-inch pieces
¼ pound medium shrimp, peeled,
   deveined
2 tablespoons minced fresh parsley
½ teaspoon Italian seasoning
¼ teaspoon cayenne pepper

Heat oil in heavy large saucepan over medium-high heat. Add onion, celery and garlic and sauté until onion is tender, about 10 minutes. Drain clams, reserving liquid. Add liquid to saucepan. Stir in tomato soup, clam juice and tomato paste and bring to boil. Add snapper, shrimp, parsley, Italian seasoning and cayenne. Simmer until shrimp are just cooked through, about 3 minutes. Stir in clams. Season with salt and pepper and serve.

Wild Rice and Mushroom Soup

4 servings

1 14½-ounce can chicken broth
½ cup wild rice

1 ounce dried shiitake mushrooms
1½ cups hot water

2 tablespoons butter
1 onion, chopped
2 garlic cloves, chopped
¼ teaspoon dried rosemary,
   crumbled

¼ teaspoon dried thyme, crumbled
1 8-ounce russet potato, peeled,
   diced
2 cups beef stock or canned beef
   broth

¾ cup (about) milk
2 tablespoons Madeira

Combine chicken broth and rice in small saucepan. Cover and simmer over medium-low heat until rice is tender and liquid is absorbed, about 50 minutes.

Meanwhile, soak mushrooms in 1½ cups hot water until soft, about 20 minutes. Drain mushrooms, reserving soaking liquid. Cut off mushroom stems and discard. Thinly slice mushrooms.

Melt 1 tablespoon butter in heavy large saucepan over medium-high heat. Add mushrooms and sauté until tender and golden brown, about 5 minutes. Transfer to small bowl. Melt remaining 1 tablespoon butter in same pan. Add onion, garlic, rosemary and thyme and sauté until onion is very tender, about 10 minutes. Mix in potato, beef stock and reserved mushroom soaking liquid. Cover and simmer until potato is very tender, about 15 minutes.

Transfer soup to blender in batches and puree until smooth. Return to saucepan. Stir in wild rice, mushrooms, ¾ cup milk and Madeira. Cover and simmer 15 minutes to blend flavors. Season with salt and pepper. (*Can be prepared 1 day ahead. Cover and refrigerate. Return soup to simmer.*) Thin with additional milk if desired and serve.

Coconut Chicken Soup

6 servings

2 14-ounce cans unsweetened coconut milk*
1 cup chicken stock or canned low-salt broth
1 cup drained canned straw mushrooms
8 ounces boneless skinless chicken breast, thinly sliced

¼ cup chopped fresh lemongrass*
1½ tablespoons minced peeled fresh ginger
1 tablespoon sugar
1½ teaspoons minced jalapeño chili
¼ cup chopped fresh cilantro
2 tablespoons fresh lime juice

Combine first 8 ingredients in heavy medium saucepan and bring to boil. Reduce heat and simmer until chicken is cooked through, about 5 minutes. Mix in chopped cilantro and lime juice. Serve.

*Available at Asian markets and some specialty foods stores.

Fresh Tomato-Corn Soup

Serve this soup with crusty French bread.

4 servings

2 cups chopped ripe plum tomatoes (about 14 ounces)
1½ cups V8 vegetable juice
1 cup frozen corn kernels, thawed
2 green onions, finely chopped
¼ cup chopped green bell pepper
2 tablespoons finely shredded fresh basil or 1 teaspoon dried, crumbled

2 large garlic cloves, minced
Hot pepper sauce (such as Tabasco)

¼ cup plain low-fat yogurt
Chopped fresh basil or parsley

Combine tomatoes and juice in large bowl. Add corn, green onions, bell pepper, 2 tablespoons basil and garlic and blend well. Season to taste with hot pepper sauce, salt and pepper. Chill at least 15 minutes and up to 2 hours.

Ladle soup into 4 bowls, dividing evenly. Garnish each with yogurt and chopped fresh basil and serve.

Cream of Garlic Soup

6 servings

3 ounces garlic cloves, peeled (about ¾ cup)
3 tablespoons olive oil
2½ cups chicken stock or canned low-salt broth
1 cup dry white wine

2½ cups milk (do not use low-fat or nonfat)
1 cup whipping cream
1 4-ounce russet potato, peeled, coarsely chopped

Blend garlic in processor to coarse paste, stopping occasionally to scrape down sides of bowl. Heat oil in heavy large saucepan over low heat. Add garlic paste and cook until just beginning to color, stirring frequently, about 12 minutes.

Add stock and wine and bring to boil. Reduce heat and simmer 30 minutes. Add milk, cream and potato and simmer 30 minutes. Puree soup in blender in batches. Return to saucepan and bring to simmer. Season to taste with salt and pepper. (*Can be prepared 1 day ahead. Cover and refrigerate. Bring to simmer before continuing.*) If soup is very thin, simmer until thickened to desired consistency. Ladle into bowls and serve.

Italian Vegetable Soup

A simple, country-style soup that's perfect for cool nights.

4 servings

3 tablespoons olive oil
1 cup chopped cabbage
1 medium onion, chopped
1 celery stalk, chopped
1 large garlic clove, minced
1½ teaspoons Italian seasoning
1½ teaspoons dried basil, crumbled
3 cups water

1½ cups tomato juice
1 10-ounce package frozen mixed vegetables
1 10-ounce package frozen chopped collard greens
1 15-ounce can cannellini (white kidney beans), drained

Heat oil in heavy large saucepan over medium heat. Add cabbage, onion, celery, garlic, Italian seasoning and basil. Sauté until vegetables are tender, about 10 minutes. Add water and tomato juice. Simmer 30 minutes. Stir in mixed vegetables, collard greens and beans. Cook until all vegetables are tender, about 10 minutes. Season to taste with salt and pepper and serve.

Tomatillo and Corn Soup

8 servings

3 tablespoons unsalted butter
1 medium onion, finely chopped
5 tomatillos,* husked, quartered
1 tablespoon minced garlic
3 10-ounce packages frozen corn kernels, thawed
4 cups chicken stock or canned low-salt broth
1 cup frozen peas, thawed

6 fresh cilantro sprigs
1 4-ounce can diced green chilies
¼ cup (packed) thawed frozen chopped spinach
1 tablespoon sugar

Tortilla chips
Sour cream
Chopped fresh cilantro

Melt butter in heavy large pot over medium-high heat. Add onion, tomatillos and garlic and sauté 5 minutes. Mix in 4 cups corn, 3 cups stock, peas and cilantro sprigs. Puree mixture in blender in batches. Return puree to pot and bring to simmer. Add chilies, spinach, sugar, remaining corn and remaining 1 cup stock to soup. Simmer 15 minutes. Season to taste with salt. (*Can be prepared 1 day ahead. Cover and refrigerate. Bring to simmer before continuing.*)

Ladle soup into bowls. Sprinkle with tortilla chips; top with sour cream and chopped cilantro. Serve immediately.

*A green vegetable (similar to a tomato) with a paper-thin husk. Available at Latin American markets, specialty foods stores and some supermarkets.

Quick Black Bean Soup

Using canned black beans makes this delicious soup a snap to prepare.

4 to 6 servings

¼ cup olive oil
1 large onion, chopped
1 red or green bell pepper, chopped
2 garlic cloves, chopped
1 14½-ounce can peeled tomatoes, chopped, juices reserved
1 4-ounce can diced green chilies
1 tablespoon dried thyme, crumbled

4 16-ounce cans black beans, drained, rinsed
2 cups (or more) canned low-salt chicken broth

Sour cream
Sliced green onions

Heat oil in heavy large saucepan over medium heat. Add onion, bell pepper and garlic and sauté until onion is tender, about 10 minutes. Mix in tomatoes with their juices, chilies and thyme. Reduce heat to low and simmer until vegetables are very soft, about 10 minutes. Add beans and 2 cups chicken broth. Puree soup in batches in processor or blender until smooth. Return soup to pot. (*Can be prepared 4 days ahead. Cover and refrigerate.*)

Bring soup to simmer. Thin with more broth if necessary. Season to taste with salt and pepper. Garnish with sour cream and sliced green onions.

❧ *Side-Dish Salads*

Eggplant, Squash and Tomato with Roasted Garlic Vinaigrette

6 servings

4 large garlic cloves, unpeeled
Olive oil
1½ tablespoons balsamic vinegar or red wine vinegar
⅓ cup olive oil

3 large Japanese eggplants, cut crosswise into ½-inch-thick rounds

3 large yellow summer squash or zucchini, cut crosswise into ½-inch-thick rounds

3 tomatoes, thinly sliced
16 fresh basil leaves, chopped

Preheat oven to 350°F. Place unpeeled garlic cloves in small baking dish. Drizzle garlic with olive oil and toss to coat. Roast garlic until very tender, about 25 minutes. Cool. Peel garlic and mince. Transfer to small bowl. Mix in balsamic vinegar. Gradually mix in ⅓ cup olive oil. Set dressing aside.

Preheat broiler. Arrange eggplant slices in single layer on broiler pan. Brush both sides with olive oil. Sprinkle with salt and pepper. Broil until beginning to brown, about 4 minutes per side. Arrange squash slices in single layer on broiler pan. Brush tops of squash with olive oil; season with salt and pepper. Broil until tops begin to brown, about 4 minutes.

Alternate eggplant and squash slices around edge of serving platter, overlapping slightly. Arrange tomato slices in center of platter. Sprinkle tomatoes with salt and pepper. Drizzle dressing over salad. (*Salad can be prepared 2 hours ahead. Cover and let stand at room temperature.*) Sprinkle with basil.

Grapefruit, Avocado and Walnut Salad

4 servings

½ cup olive oil
3 tablespoons red wine vinegar
1 large garlic clove, pressed
1 teaspoon honey
½ teaspoon Worcestershire sauce
½ teaspoon dried tarragon, crumbled
½ teaspoon dry mustard

1 pink grapefruit
1 head butter lettuce, separated into leaves
1 avocado, sliced
½ cup toasted walnuts

For dressing, combine first 7 ingredients in small bowl. Season dressing to taste with salt and pepper.

Using small sharp knife, remove peel and white pith from grapefruit. Working over large bowl to catch juices, cut between membranes to release segments. Place lettuce on large plate. Arrange grapefruit sections and avocado decoratively atop lettuce. Drizzle salad with enough dressing to season to taste. Sprinkle with walnuts and serve.

Spinach Salad with Hearts of Palm

10 servings

3 tablespoons red wine vinegar
2 teaspoons Dijon mustard
1 teaspoon sugar
⅓ cup olive oil

2 pounds fresh spinach, stems trimmed
1 14-ounce can hearts of palm, drained, sliced
1½ teaspoons grated lemon peel

Whisk first 3 ingredients in small bowl. Gradually whisk in oil. Season to taste with salt and pepper. (*Dressing can be prepared 1 day ahead. Cover dressing and let stand at room temperature.*)

Combine spinach, hearts of palm and lemon peel in bowl. Add enough dressing to season to taste and toss gently. Divide among plates and serve.

Sliced Tomatoes with Pesto

10 servings

1 cup firmly packed fresh parsley
1 cup loosely packed fresh basil leaves
½ cup chopped onion
2 garlic cloves, chopped
½ cup olive oil

6 large tomatoes, cut into ⅓-inch-thick slices
1 tablespoon minced lemon peel (yellow part only)

Finely chop fresh parsley, basil, onion and garlic in processor. With machine running, gradually add olive oil and blend until smooth. Season with salt and pepper. (*Pesto can be prepared 1 day ahead. Cover and refrigerate.*)

Arrange tomatoes on platter. Sprinkle with peel. Top each tomato slice with ½ teaspoon pesto. Let stand 30 minutes at room temperature before serving.

Arugula Salad with Baked Goat Cheese

6 servings

2 6-ounce logs soft fresh goat cheese (such as Montrachet), cut into ½-inch-thick rounds
2 tablespoons chopped fresh parsley
1 tablespoon minced fresh oregano or 1 teaspoon dried, crumbled
1 tablespoon minced fresh tarragon or 1 teaspoon dried, crumbled

2 tablespoons chopped green onions
½ cup extra-virgin olive oil
1 cup dry coarse breadcrumbs
2½ tablespoons balsamic vinegar or red wine vinegar
4 bunches fresh arugula, stemmed

Place cheese in baking dish. Sprinkle half of herbs and green onions over. Turn and sprinkle remaining herbs and onions over. Drizzle ¼ cup oil over. Season to taste with salt and pepper. Let stand 1 hour at room temperature.

Preheat oven to 350°F. Dredge goat cheese rounds in breadcrumbs. Transfer to baking sheet. Bake until soft, about 10 minutes.

Meanwhile, whisk vinegar and remaining ¼ cup oil in small bowl. Season to taste with salt and pepper. Place arugula in medium bowl. Toss with enough dressing to season to taste. Divide greens among plates. Top with goat cheese.

Green Bean, Potato and Leek Salad

6 servings

8 medium-small red potatoes
1 pound green beans, trimmed, halved crosswise
1 tablespoon Dijon mustard
3 tablespoons white wine vinegar
½ cup vegetable oil

2 tablespoons (¼ stick) butter
4 leeks (white part only), halved lengthwise, thinly sliced crosswise

Chopped fresh parsley
3 hard-boiled eggs, shelled, quartered (optional)

Boil or steam potatoes and green beans separately until tender but not mushy. Drain or remove from steamer. Cut each potato into eighths. Place in salad bowl. Add green beans. Blend Dijon mustard and vinegar in small bowl. Whisk in vegetable oil in thin stream. Pour over potatoes and beans and mix gently to coat. Season salad to taste with salt and pepper. Set aside.

Melt 2 tablespoons butter in heavy large skillet over medium heat. Add leeks and sauté until tender and lightly browned, about 7 minutes.

Divide potato and green bean mixture among salad plates. Top each with sautéed leeks. Sprinkle salads with chopped fresh parsley. Garnish each salad with 2 hard-boiled egg quarters, if desired, and serve.

Watercress and Orange Salad

6 servings

2 medium oranges
½ cup vegetable oil
¼ cup olive oil
¼ cup raspberry vinegar or red wine
  vinegar
2 medium shallots, minced

3 bunches watercress, ends
  trimmed

Using small sharp knife, cut peel and white pith from oranges. Cut oranges crosswise into ½-inch-thick rounds. Cut each round into quarters. Transfer to large bowl. Whisk both oils, vinegar and shallots in small bowl. Season to taste with salt and pepper. (*Can be prepared 8 hours ahead. Cover and chill oranges. Store vinaigrette at room temperature.*)

Add watercress to oranges. Add enough vinaigrette to season to taste and toss well. Divide among plates and serve.

Parslied Potato Salad

10 servings

1 large onion, finely chopped
¾ cup cold water

7 large russet potatoes, halved
3 hard-boiled eggs, peeled, chopped
1 cup chopped fresh parsley

1 cup regular or reduced-calorie
  mayonnaise
¼ cup white wine vinegar
1 teaspoon celery seed

Combine onion and water in small bowl and let stand 1 hour.

Cook potatoes in large pot of boiling salted water until tender. Drain and cool. Peel potatoes and cut into 1-inch cubes. Drain onion. Combine onion, potatoes, eggs and parsley in large bowl. Whisk mayonnaise, vinegar and celery seed in small bowl. Pour over potato salad and toss to combine. Cover and refrigerate at least 2 hours.

Cabbage, Snow Pea and Carrot Slaw

A slaw with a difference—color from peas, crunch from nuts and spice from cumin and cayenne.

4 servings

¼ head green cabbage, cored, very
  thinly sliced
6 ounces snow peas, stringed,
  halved lengthwise
3 large carrots, peeled, halved
  lengthwise, cut into 2½-inch-long
  pieces and thinly sliced

1 tablespoon cider vinegar
3 tablespoons olive oil
1 teaspoon ground cumin
⅛ teaspoon (scant) cayenne pepper
⅓ cup chopped walnuts

Combine first 3 ingredients in large bowl. Place vinegar in small bowl. Gradually mix in oil. Add cumin and cayenne. Mix dressing into slaw. Season to taste with salt and pepper. (*Can be prepared 2 hours ahead. Cover and refrigerate.*) Sprinkle slaw with chopped walnuts and serve.

Morton's Caesar Salad

A specialty at Morton's restaurant in Chicago.

4 servings

¾ cup olive oil
¼ cup red wine vinegar
6 anchovy fillets, minced
4 teaspoons minced garlic
1 tablespoon fresh lemon juice
1 tablespoon Dijon mustard
1 teaspoon white pepper

1 cup grated Parmesan cheese (about 3 ounces)
1 large head romaine lettuce, torn into bite-size pieces
Additional grated Parmesan cheese
Croutons

Blend first 7 ingredients in processor. Add 1 cup grated Parmesan cheese and blend until combined. Season to taste with salt. (*Can be prepared 2 days ahead. Cover and refrigerate. Bring to room temperature and whisk to blend before using.*) Place lettuce in large bowl. Add enough dressing to season to taste and toss well. Divide salad among plates. Sprinkle with additional Parmesan cheese. Top salad with croutons and serve.

Fennel, Watercress and Parmesan Salad

4 servings

¼ cup olive oil
3 tablespoons balsamic vinegar or red wine vinegar
2 tablespoons grated Parmesan cheese
½ teaspoon chopped fennel seeds
1 large fennel bulb, trimmed, thinly sliced

1 large bunch watercress, stems trimmed
1 small head radicchio, sliced

1 4-ounce piece Parmesan cheese

Whisk oil, vinegar, 2 tablespoons cheese and fennel seeds together in small bowl. Season to taste with salt and pepper. Toss sliced fennel, watercress and radicchio in bowl. (*Can be prepared 8 hours ahead. Cover dressing and greens separately. Refrigerate greens.*)

Using vegetable peeler, cut 4 ounces cheese into strips. Whisk dressing to blend. Pour enough over greens to coat lightly. Add cheese strips and toss. Serve, passing remaining dressing separately.

Bulgur Salad with Oriental Dressing

4 servings

2 cups water
1 cup bulgur wheat*
1 cup thinly sliced red cabbage
1 cup coarsely grated peeled carrots
1 cup seedless red grapes
½ cup chopped red bell pepper
½ cup chopped green onions
½ cup chopped fresh parsley

⅓ cup rice vinegar
2 tablespoons peanut oil
1 tablespoon soy sauce
1 tablespoon oriental sesame oil
1 tablespoon sesame seeds, toasted
1 teaspoon Dijon mustard

Bring 2 cups water to boil in medium saucepan. Stir in bulgur. Cover and remove from heat. Let stand until softened, about 15 minutes. Drain bulgur;

transfer to large bowl. Add cabbage, carrots, grapes, bell pepper, green onions and parsley; toss to combine.

Blend vinegar, peanut oil, soy, sesame oil, sesame seeds and mustard in blender until smooth. Pour over salad and toss to coat. Cover and refrigerate until well chilled. (*Can be prepared 1 day ahead; keep refrigerated.*)

*Bulgur wheat, also called cracked wheat, is available at natural foods stores and supermarkets.

Saffron-roasted Potato and Fennel Salad

4 servings

1½ **pounds medium red potatoes (unpeeled), each cut into 8 wedges**
2 **tablespoons minced garlic**
2 **teaspoons chopped fresh thyme or ½ teaspoon dried, crumbled**
2 **teaspoons chopped fresh rosemary or ½ teaspoon dried, crumbled**

½ **teaspoon saffron threads, crumbled**
½ **cup olive oil**

1 **fennel bulb, trimmed, sliced**
1 **tablespoon fresh lemon juice**

Preheat oven to 400°F. Combine first 5 ingredients in medium bowl. Mix in ¼ cup oil. Season with salt and pepper. Transfer mixture to baking pan. Cover and bake 15 minutes. Uncover, stir potatoes and bake until tender, about 20 minutes more. Transfer potato mixture to bowl and cool.

Mix fennel, lemon juice and ¼ cup oil with potatoes. Season with salt and pepper. (*Can be made 4 hours ahead. Let stand at room temperature.*)

❦ *Main-Dish Salads*

Wild Rice and Chicken Salad with Tarragon

2 to 4 servings

1 **14½-ounce can chicken broth**
½ **cup wild rice (about 3 ounces)**

2 **cups diced cooked chicken (about 9 ounces)**
1 **large celery stalk, diced**
½ **large crisp red apple, diced**
1 **green onion, thinly sliced**

2 **tablespoons minced fresh tarragon or 2 teaspoons dried, crumbled**
2½ **tablespoons olive oil**
1½ **tablespoons tarragon vinegar**
1 **teaspoon Dijon mustard**
Pinch of sugar

Combine broth and wild rice in small saucepan. Bring to boil. Cover and simmer over medium-low heat until rice is tender and liquid is absorbed, about 50 minutes. Transfer to medium bowl. Cover and refrigerate until well chilled.

Add chicken, celery, apple, green onion and tarragon to wild rice. Whisk remaining ingredients to blend in small bowl. Pour over wild rice mixture and toss well. Season with salt and pepper.

Sesame Steak Salad

4 servings

Dressing

- ¹/₃ cup soy sauce
- ¹/₄ cup rice wine vinegar
- 2 tablespoons vegetable oil
- 1 tablespoon oriental sesame oil
- 2 garlic cloves, minced
- 2 teaspoons finely grated peeled fresh ginger
- 1 teaspoon chili oil*
- 1 teaspoon sugar

Salad

- 8 asparagus stalks, trimmed, cut into 1-inch pieces
- 8 large broccoli florets
- 12 ounces thinly sliced rare roast beef, cut into 3 × 1-inch strips
- ¹/₂ head savoy cabbage, shredded
- ¹/₂ large green bell pepper, thinly sliced
- 2 green onions, chopped

For dressing: Whisk all ingredients together in medium bowl.

For salad: Cook asparagus in large saucepan of boiling salted water until just crisp-tender. Drain. Refresh under cold water. Drain well. Repeat process with broccoli florets.

Place beef in large bowl. Add dressing and marinate 5 minutes.

Line platter with cabbage. Place asparagus and broccoli in center of salad. Using tongs, remove beef from dressing. Arrange beef and bell pepper around edge of platter. Pour dressing over salad. Garnish with green onions.

*Available in Asian markets and in the Asian section of many supermarkets.

Chinese Chicken Salad

6 servings

Vegetable oil (for deep frying)
- 2 ounces maifun (rice stick) noodles*

- 6 tablespoons rice vinegar
- 2¹/₂ tablespoons soy sauce
- 2 garlic cloves, minced
- 2 teaspoons wasabi powder*
- ¹/₂ teaspoon dried crushed red pepper
- ³/₄ cup peanut oil
- 3 tablespoons oriental sesame oil

- 1¹/₂ pounds boneless skinless chicken breasts, cut crosswise into ¹/₂-inch-wide strips
- 1 head romaine lettuce, torn into bite-size pieces
- 2 red or green bell peppers, cut into matchstick-size strips
- ¹/₄ cup chopped fresh cilantro
- ¹/₄ cup chopped fresh basil
- ¹/₄ cup chopped fresh mint leaves

Heat oil in heavy large saucepan to 350°F. Add noodles and cook until puffed and crisp, about 5 seconds; do not let brown. Using slotted spoon, transfer noodles to paper towels.

Whisk rice vinegar, soy sauce, garlic, wasabi and red pepper in medium bowl. Gradually whisk in both oils.

Heat ¹/₄ cup dressing in heavy large skillet over high heat. Add chicken and sauté until cooked through, about 5 minutes. Transfer chicken to small bowl. Cover and refrigerate until well chilled. (*Can be prepared 4 hours ahead. Let noodles stand at room temperature. Keep chicken refrigerated.*)

Combine noodles, chicken, lettuce, bell peppers and herbs in large bowl. Toss with enough remaining dressing to season to taste. Divide salad among plates and serve immediately.

*Available at Asian markets, specialty foods stores and some supermarkets.

Shrimp, Orange and Olive Salad with Sherry Vinaigrette

6 servings

¼ cup plus 2 tablespoons olive oil
3 tablespoons Sherry wine vinegar
   or red wine vinegar
1 garlic clove, pressed
1 teaspoon sugar
1 teaspoon grated orange peel
2 oranges

1 pound medium cooked shrimp,
   peeled, deveined
1 cup sliced green olives

8 cups mixed baby lettuces
2 green onions, minced

Whisk first 5 ingredients in large bowl for dressing. Season to taste with salt and pepper. Cut peel and white pith from oranges. Quarter oranges lengthwise, then slice crosswise. Add oranges, shrimp and olives to dressing. Refrigerate 1 hour.
   Add lettuces and green onions to dressing mixture and toss well.

Beef Tenderloin Salad

6 servings

1 tablespoon vegetable oil
1½ pounds 1-inch-thick beef
   tenderloin steaks (about 6 steaks)

Dressing
1¼ cups olive oil
⅓ cup balsamic vinegar or red wine
   vinegar
3 tablespoons chopped fresh chives
2 tablespoons orange juice
1 tablespoon poppy seeds

Salad
¾ cup green beans, trimmed
1 head Bibb lettuce, torn into bite-
   size pieces

1 head red leaf lettuce, torn into
   bite-size pieces
1 16-ounce can mandarin oranges,
   drained
1 cup crumbled feta cheese (about
   4 ounces)
¾ cup coarsely chopped walnuts
   (about 3 ounces)
½ medium-size red onion, thinly
   sliced into rings

Heat oil in heavy large skillet over medium-high heat. Season steaks with pepper. Add to skillet and cook to desired doneness, about 5 minutes per side for medium-rare. Transfer steaks to platter. Let stand until cool, about 15 minutes. Cover and refrigerate until well chilled.
   For dressing: Whisk all ingredients in medium bowl to blend. Season to taste with salt and pepper.
   For salad: Cook green beans in large saucepan of boiling salted water until just crisp-tender. Drain. Refresh under cold water. Drain well. Pat dry. Combine green beans and remaining ingredients in large bowl. Cut steaks diagonally into thin slices. Add to salad. Add dressing and toss to coat; serve.

Roasted Chicken, Bell Pepper and Onion Salad

8 servings

Chicken and Vegetables
- ²/₃ cup olive oil
- ²/₃ cup balsamic vinegar or red wine vinegar
- ¼ cup chopped fresh rosemary or 2 tablespoons dried, crumbled
- 5 garlic cloves, minced
- ½ teaspoon dried crushed red pepper
- 4 pounds chicken breast halves
- 3 large red bell peppers, cut into ½-inch-wide strips
- 2 large yellow bell peppers, cut into ½-inch-wide strips
- 3 large red onions, cut into ½-inch-thick rounds

Dressing
- 2 teaspoons Dijon mustard
- 2 teaspoons balsamic vinegar or red wine vinegar
- ¼ cup olive oil
- 4 teaspoons grated orange peel
- 1 teaspoon chopped fresh rosemary or ½ teaspoon dried, crumbled

Ornamental kale leaves
Fresh rosemary sprigs

For chicken and vegetables: Preheat oven to 425°F. Combine first 5 ingredients in medium bowl. Place chicken breasts in large baking pan. Divide vegetables among 2 large baking pans. Brush chicken on both sides with oil mixture. Sprinkle both sides with salt and pepper. Arrange skin side up in pan. Divide remaining oil mixture between pans of vegetables; mix to coat vegetables. Sprinkle with salt and pepper. Bake chicken until just cooked through, about 35 minutes, and vegetables until edges brown, about 40 minutes. Cool slightly.

For dressing: Combine mustard and vinegar in medium bowl. Gradually mix in oil. Add grated orange peel and chopped rosemary.

Remove skin and bones from chicken. Cut chicken into ½-inch-wide strips. Add to dressing and mix to coat. Season to taste with salt and pepper. Mix with roasted vegetables in large bowl. Season entire salad to taste with salt and pepper. (*Can be prepared 1 day ahead. Cover and refrigerate.*)

Line platter with kale. Spoon salad over. Garnish with rosemary sprigs.

3 ❦ *Pasta, Pizza and Sandwiches*

If you stood on a corner and took a random poll of favorite foods, chances are pasta, pizza and sandwiches would all rank up there very near the top. As that familiar advertising slogan goes, nobody doesn't like these three: They're great-tasting, comforting foods, and we offer a tempting selection of recipes for each here.

When it comes to lasagne, the richer the better, and the Fontina, Mushroom and Pancetta Lasagne, made with a delicious Tomato, Porcini and Pancetta Sauce, fills that bill perfectly. For something on the lighter side, try Pasta with Sugar Snap Peas, Asparagus and Parmesan. If you love ravioli but can't spare the time it usually takes to make it, there's Salmon Ravioli with Basil Cream Sauce, made fast and easy with purchased wonton wrappers. Sometimes, the easiest pasta of all is a baked casserole, such as Oven-baked Ziti with Three Cheeses, which can be made ahead and popped in the oven just before serving.

For the creative pizza lover, there's Pizza Picasso, using the baked cheese pizza crusts available in supermarkets, served up with a variety of toppings and sauces to mix and match as you please. For a different take on pizza, try Mexican Pizza, taco-seasoned ground beef and other ingredients sandwiched between flour tortillas and cut into wedges.

And speaking of sandwiches, there are several surprises in the pages that follow, including BLT & G(uacamole), with guacamole replacing the usual mayo, and Fried Prosciutto and Cheese Sandwiches, definitely not your ordinary ham and cheese.

❦ *Pasta*

Fontina, Mushroom and Pancetta Lasagne

8 servings

Filling
2 15-ounce containers ricotta cheese
1 10-ounce package frozen chopped spinach, cooked according to package directions, drained, squeezed dry
½ cup grated Parmesan cheese (about 1½ ounces)
2 eggs

Mushrooms
1 tablespoon olive oil
2 ounces pancetta* or bacon, chopped
2 teaspoons minced fresh rosemary or 1 teaspoon dried, crumbled
12 ounces button mushrooms, sliced

Assembly
12 (about) lasagne noodles

Tomato, Porcini and Pancetta Sauce (see recipe)
1 pound Fontina cheese, grated
¾ cup grated Parmesan cheese (about 3 ounces)

1 tomato, seeded, chopped
2 teaspoons minced fresh rosemary or 1 teaspoon dried, crumbled

For filling: Combine first 3 ingredients in large bowl. Season with salt and pepper. Add eggs and mix well. (*Can be prepared 1 day ahead. Cover and chill.*)

For mushrooms: Heat oil in heavy large skillet over medium heat. Add pancetta and rosemary and cook 3 minutes to render fat. Add mushrooms, season with salt and pepper and cook until juices evaporate, stirring frequently, approximately 12 minutes.

Assembly: Cook noodles in large pot of boiling salted water until just tender but still firm to bite, stirring occasionally. Drain. Rinse under cold water to cool; drain noodles well.

Oil 13 × 9 × 2-inch baking dish. Spread 1 cup Tomato, Porcini and Pancetta Sauce over bottom of dish. Arrange 3 to 4 noodles over, trimming to fit as necessary. Spread half of ricotta filling over. Spoon 1 cup sauce over. Sprinkle with 1 cup Fontina and ¼ cup Parmesan cheese. Top with 3 to 4 noodles, trimming to fit. Spread remaining ricotta filling over noodles. Spoon 1 cup sauce over. Sprinkle with 1 cup Fontina and ¼ cup Parmesan. Reserve ½ cup sautéed mushrooms for garnish. Spread remaining mushrooms over cheese. Arrange remaining noodles over. Spread remaining sauce over noodles. Sprinkle remaining Fontina and ¼ cup Parmesan over. Cover with foil. (*Can be prepared 1 day ahead. Refrigerate lasagne and reserved ½ cup mushrooms separately. Let lasagne stand 2 hours at room temperature before continuing.*)

Preheat oven to 350°F. Bake covered lasagne 30 minutes. Uncover and continue baking until bubbling and cheese melts, about 20 minutes. Arrange reserved ½ cup mushrooms, tomato and 2 teaspoons rosemary over. Let stand 10 minutes. Cut into squares and serve.

Tomato, Porcini and Pancetta Sauce

Makes about 4 cups

1 ⅞- to 1-ounce package dried
  porcini mushrooms*
1 cup hot water

1 tablespoon olive oil
2 ounces pancetta* or bacon,
  chopped

1 medium onion, chopped
2 teaspoons minced fresh rosemary
  or 1 teaspoon dried, crumbled
⅛ teaspoon dried crushed red
  pepper
1 28-ounce can crushed tomatoes
  with added puree

Rinse mushrooms briefly under cold water. Place in small bowl. Pour 1 cup hot water over and let soak 30 minutes to soften. Remove mushrooms from water; reserve soaking waer. Cut hard stems from mushrooms.

Heat oil in heavy medium saucepan over medium heat. Add pancetta and sauté 2 minutes. Add onion and rosemary and cook until onion is translucent, stirring occasionally, about 8 minutes. Add dried red pepper and sauté 20 seconds. Add tomatoes and mushrooms. Carefully pour in reserved mushroom soaking liquid, leaving sediment in bowl. Simmer until sauce is thick, stirring occasionally, about 35 minutes. Season with salt and pepper. (*Can be prepared 1 day ahead. Cover and chill.*)

*Pancetta, which is Italian unsmoked bacon cured in salt, and porcini mushrooms are available at Italian markets and some specialty foods stores.

Pasta with Sugar Snap Peas, Asparagus and Parmesan

4 servings

1 pound asparagus, trimmed, cut
  into 1½-inch pieces
½ pound farfalle (bow-tie) pasta
½ pound sugar snap peas or snow
  peas, trimmed

3 tablespoons olive oil
½ cup grated Parmesan cheese
  (about 1½ ounces)
  Additional grated
  Parmesan cheese

Add asparagus to large pot of boiling salted water. Cook until just crisp-tender. Transfer to bowl of cold water using slotted spoon. Cool asparagus slightly and drain. Add pasta to same pot of water and boil until just tender but still firm to bite. Add sugar snap peas and boil 2 minutes. Add asparagus and heat through. Drain well. Return pasta-vegetable mixture to pot. Add oil and toss to coat. Add ½ cup cheese. Season with salt and pepper. Serve immediately, passing additional cheese separately.

Couscous with Green Onions

Couscous is a small grain-shaped pasta that is used frequently in Middle Eastern cooking. You can find it at many supermarkets and specialty foods stores.

6 servings

2 tablespoons (¼ stick) butter
2 tablespoons olive oil
3 green onions, minced

2½ cups canned low-salt chicken
  broth
2 cups couscous
  Chopped fresh parsley

Melt butter with oil in heavy medium saucepan over medium heat. Add onions and sauté 1 minute. Add broth and bring to boil. Mix in couscous. Remove from heat. Cover and let stand 10 minutes. Fluff couscous with fork. Season with salt. Transfer to bowl. Top with parsley.

Fettuccine with Brie and Bacon Sauce

6 servings

½ pound bacon, chopped
½ cup half and half
½ cup canned low-salt chicken broth
1 cup (about 4 ounces) grated Parmesan cheese

1 teaspoon cracked pepper
3 ounces Brie cheese, rind removed, thinly sliced
16 ounces fettuccine

Cook bacon in heavy large skillet over medium heat until fat is rendered and bacon begins to brown, about 6 minutes. Using slotted spoon, transfer bacon to plate. Discard fat from skillet. Add half and half and chicken broth to same skillet and bring to boil over medium heat. Gradually add Parmesan and stir until cheese melts. Add pepper and bacon. Reduce heat to low and gradually add Brie, stirring until cheese melts.

Meanwhile, cook fettuccine in large pot of boiling salted water until just tender but still firm to bite. Drain well. Add fettuccine to sauce in skillet. Toss until coated with sauce. Divide fettuccine among plates and serve.

Angel Hair Frittata

An Italian dish that's great with brunch, or as a light lunch or appetizer.

4 servings

4 tablespoons olive oil
2 small zucchini, sliced
1 tomato, seeded, chopped
2 large mushrooms, sliced
1 green onion, sliced
4 garlic cloves, minced
2 tablespoons chopped black olives
¼ teaspoon dried basil, crumbled

⅛ teaspoon dried oregano, crumbled

4 eggs
1½ cups grated Romano cheese
6 ounces angel hair pasta, freshly cooked
Additional grated Romano cheese
2 tomatoes, chopped

Heat 2 tablespoons oil in heavy medium skillet over medium-high heat. Add zucchini, 1 tomato, mushrooms, onion and garlic and sauté until tender, about 3 minutes. Add olives and herbs. Cool.

Preheat broiler. Beat eggs and 1½ cups cheese in large bowl. Season with salt and pepper. Mix in vegetables and pasta. Heat remaining 2 tablespoons oil in heavy large broilerproof skillet over medium heat. Add egg mixture to skillet. Press mixture with back of spatula to even thickness. Cook until frittata is set and golden brown on bottom. Transfer skillet to broiler and cook until top of frittata is set, about 2 minutes. Run small knife around edge of frittata to loosen. Invert skillet onto large plate. Remove skillet. Cut frittata into wedges. Serve, passing additional cheese and chopped tomatoes separately.

Pasta with Pesto Sauce, Macadamia Nuts and Roasted Peppers

4 servings

3 cups loosely packed fresh basil
   leaves (about 2 ounces)
1 cup olive oil
¾ cup roasted macadamia nuts
   (3 ounces)
6 garlic cloves, minced
1¼ cups grated Parmesan cheese
   (about 5 ounces)

2 large red bell peppers

1 pound linguine
2 tablespoons olive oil
   Chopped macadamia nuts
   Additional grated Parmesan
   cheese

Puree first 4 ingredients in processor. Transfer sauce to large bowl. Stir in 1¼ cups Parmesan cheese. Season pesto to taste with salt and pepper. (*Can be prepared 1 week ahead. Transfer to jar. Pour enough additional oil over pesto to cover completely. Cover and refrigerate. Pour off extra oil before using.*)

Char peppers over gas flame or in broiler until blackened. Wrap in paper bag and let steam 15 minutes. Peel and seed; slice peppers thinly.

Cook linguine in large pot of boiling salted water until just tender but still firm to bite, stirring occasionally. Drain well. Return to same pot and mix with 2 tablespoons olive oil. Divide pasta among plates. Spoon pesto sauce over. Garnish with roasted peppers, chopped nuts and additional Parmesan.

Oven-baked Ziti with Three Cheeses

A delicious take on lasagne, made with tube-shaped pasta instead.

6 servings

2 tablespoons olive oil
1 onion, chopped
2 large garlic cloves, chopped
1 teaspoon fennel seeds
⅓ cup tomato paste
1 8-ounce can tomato sauce
1 cup water
1 teaspoon dried oregano,
   crumbled

½ teaspoon dried rubbed sage
½ cup grated Parmesan cheese

1 15-ounce container ricotta cheese
1 egg
8 ounces mozzarella cheese, grated

12 ounces freshly cooked ziti or
   other tubular pasta

Heat oil in heavy large saucepan over medium-low heat. Add onion, garlic and fennel seeds and sauté until translucent, about 5 minutes. Mix in tomato paste and cook 1 minute. Add tomato sauce, water, oregano and sage. Simmer until mixture thickens slightly, stirring occasionally, about 10 minutes. Stir in ¼ cup Parmesan. Season to taste with salt and pepper.

Preheat oven to 450°F. Butter 9 × 13-inch glass baking dish. In medium bowl combine ricotta cheese and egg. Reserve ¼ cup mozzarella cheese for topping. Add remaining mozzarella to ricotta cheese mixture and blend. Season mixture with salt and pepper.

Spread ¼ of tomato sauce over bottom of prepared dish. Layer ⅓ of pasta over. Drop half of ricotta cheese mixture over by spoonfuls. Spread ¼ of sauce over. Repeat layering with another ⅓ of pasta, remaining cheese mixture, ¼ of sauce and remaining pasta. Spread remaining sauce over and sprinkle with reserved mozzarella and remaining ¼ cup Parmesan. (*Can be prepared 1 day ahead. Cover and refrigerate.*)

Cover casserole and bake until heated through, about 40 minutes.

Salmon Ravioli with Basil Cream Sauce

Purchased wonton wrappers make this a fast and easy ravioli.

4 servings

Ravioli
  Cornstarch
6 ounces barbecued salmon (such as Lasco brand)
4 ounces cream cheese
2 teaspoons fresh lemon juice
⅛ teaspoon white pepper

32 wonton wrappers
1 egg white, beaten to blend

Sauce
1 cup firmly packed fresh basil leaves
¼ cup olive oil
1 tablespoon pine nuts
2 garlic cloves
¼ teaspoon white pepper
1 cup half and half
½ cup whipping cream
1 cup grated Romano cheese (about 4 ounces)

For ravioli: Line baking sheet with waxed paper. Sprinkle with cornstarch. Remove skin and bones from salmon. Place salmon in processor. Add cream cheese, fresh lemon juice and white pepper and blend well. (*Can be prepared 1 day ahead; cover filling and refrigerate.*)

Place 1 wonton wrapper on work surface. Place 1 rounded teaspoon filling in center of wonton. Brush edges with egg white. Fold wonton diagonally in half, enclosing filling and forming triangle. Gently press to remove any air bubbles and seal edges. Place on prepared baking sheet. Repeat with remaining wontons, filling and egg white. (*Can be prepared 2 hours ahead. Cover with plastic wrap and refrigerate.*)

For sauce: Blend first 5 ingredients in processor until basil is finely chopped. Bring half and half and cream to simmer in heavy medium saucepan. Whisk in basil mixture and cheese and bring to simmer. (*Can be made 2 hours ahead. Cover and let stand at room temperature. Bring to simmer before using.*)

Cook ravioli in batches in large pot of boiling salted water until just tender, about 3 minutes per batch. Transfer ravioli to plates using slotted spoon. Spoon sauce over and serve immediately.

Cajun Fettuccine

A robust take on a great Italian staple.

6 servings

2 tablespoons vegetable oil
1 onion, chopped
3 large garlic cloves, chopped
1 tablespoon Cajun or Creole seasoning
2 cups sliced fresh mushrooms (about 5½ ounces)
2 cups canned ready-cut peeled tomatoes with juices (about 1½ 16-ounce cans)

1½ cups tomato juice
1 cup frozen peas
1 small zucchini, chopped
½ cup chopped drained roasted red peppers in jar
36 small clams
12 ounces fettuccine, freshly cooked
½ cup grated Parmesan cheese

Heat oil in large skillet over medium-high heat. Add onion, garlic and Cajun seasoning. Sauté until slightly softened, about 5 minutes. Stir in mushrooms and cook until wilted, about 4 minutes. Add tomatoes and tomato juice. Simmer 15 minutes. Stir in peas, zucchini, peppers and clams. Cover and cook until clams open, about 8 minutes. Discard any clams that do not open. Season sauce to taste with salt and pepper. Place pasta in large bowl. Add sauce and stir to coat. Sprinkle with Parmesan cheese and serve.

Sun-dried Tomato Spaghetti

4 servings

1 cup dry-pack sun-dried tomatoes
½ cup olive oil
4 garlic cloves, minced
½ teaspoon dried crushed red pepper

1 pound spaghetti, freshly cooked
1 cup grated Parmesan cheese
½ cup toasted pine nuts
Additional grated Parmesan cheese

Place sun-dried tomatoes in small bowl. Add enough boiling water to just cover tomatoes. Let stand until soft, about 1 minute. Drain. Coarsely chop tomatoes.

Heat olive oil in heavy small skillet. Add sun-dried tomatoes, garlic and dried crushed red pepper. Sauté until garlic is just golden, about 3 minutes. Transfer mixture to large bowl. Add spaghetti and 1 cup Parmesan. Toss well. Sprinkle with pine nuts. Serve, passing additional Parmesan separately.

❧ *Pizza*

Pizza Picasso

This was named after the artist because diners are presented with a variety of sauces and toppings so that they can design their own abstract-looking pizzas. Bobolis are available in most major supermarkets.

6 servings

Red Bell Pepper and Tomato Sauce (see recipe)
Pesto Sauce (see recipe)
Olive-Anchovy Sauce (see recipe)
8 ounces smoked chicken, diced
8 ounces pepperoni, thinly sliced
8 ounces mozzarella cheese, shredded

8 ounces provolone cheese, shredded
3 ounces Parmesan cheese, grated
3 ounces Romano cheese, grated
4 ounces prosciutto slices, chopped
6 medium Bobolis (baked cheese pizza crusts)

Preheat oven to 425°F. Place first 10 ingredients in separate bowls on counter. Set out Boboli crusts and allow guests to assemble their own pizzas, using sauces and toppings of their choice. Place pizzas on baking sheets. Bake until cheeses melt and crusts are crisp, about 20 minutes.

Red Bell Pepper and Tomato Sauce

Makes about 1¾ cups

1 8-ounce can tomato sauce
1 7-ounce jar roasted red bell peppers, drained
2 tablespoons fresh oregano leaves or 2 teaspoons dried, crumbled

2 tablespoons dry red wine
⅛ teaspoon cayenne pepper
2 tablespoons olive oil

Puree first 5 ingredients in processor. Mix in oil. Season with salt and pepper. (*Can be made 2 days ahead. Cover and refrigerate.*)

Pesto Sauce

Makes about 1⅓ cups

4 cups lightly packed fresh basil
   leaves
½ cup toasted pine nuts
6 garlic cloves
½ cup olive oil
1 tablespoon unsalted butter, room
   temperature

½ cup grated Parmesan cheese
¼ cup grated Romano cheese
1 teaspoon fresh lemon juice
⅛ teaspoon white pepper

Finely grind basil, nuts and garlic in processor. Gradually blend in oil, then butter. Add both cheeses, lemon juice and white pepper and blend well. Season with salt. (*Can be prepared 1 week ahead. Place in container. Top with a thin layer of olive oil to seal; cover and refrigerate.*)

Olive-Anchovy Sauce

Makes about 1¼ cups

1½ cups black Kalamata* olives
   (about 9 ounces), pitted
6 tablespoons olive oil

4 anchovy fillets
1½ tablespoons fresh lemon juice

Blend all ingredients to coarse puree in processor. Season to taste with pepper. (*Can be prepared 2 days ahead. Cover and refrigerate. Stir well before using.*)

*Black, brine-cured olives, available at Greek and Italian markets and some supermarkets.

Triple Cheese Pizza

4 servings

1 16-ounce Boboli (baked cheese
   pizza crust)
6 tablespoons purchased pesto
   sauce
1 cup grated Fontina cheese (about
   4 ounces)
5 plum tomatoes, seeded, thinly
   sliced

2 teaspoons dried oregano,
   crumbled
½ cup grated mozzarella cheese
   (about 2 ounces)
¼ cup grated Parmesan cheese
   Fresh basil leaves (optional)

Preheat oven to 500°F. Place pizza crust on large baking sheet. Spread pesto over. Sprinkle evenly with Fontina cheese. Arrange tomato slices over. Season with pepper. Sprinkle oregano over, then mozzarella and Parmesan cheeses. Bake until crust is golden brown and topping bubbles, about 10 minutes. Garnish with basil leaves and serve immediately.

Tricolor Boboli Pizzas

6 servings

¼ cup olive oil
2 large red onions, sliced
2 large red bell peppers, thinly sliced

2 1-pound Bobolis (baked cheese pizza crusts)
¾ cup olive paste (olivada)*

½ pound soft fresh goat cheese (such as Montrachet), crumbled
½ cup chopped fresh oregano
½ cup toasted pine nuts (about 3 ounces)

Heat olive oil in heavy large skillet over medium heat. Add sliced red onions and sliced red bell peppers and sauté until beginning to brown, stirring frequently, about 10 minutes. (*Can be made 4 hours ahead. Let stand at room temperature.*)

Preheat oven to 450°F. Place Bobolis on pizza pans or cookie sheets. Spread each Boboli with half of olive paste. Top each with half of onion mixture. Sprinkle with crumbled goat cheese. Bake until cheese softens, about 10 minutes. Remove from oven. Sprinkle with chopped fresh oregano and toasted pine nuts. Cut pizzas into wedges and serve.

*An olive spread available at Italian markets and specialty foods stores. If unavailable, use pureed, pitted, brine-cured black olives, such as Kalamata.

Quick Sausage Pizzas

2 servings

2 tablespoons olive oil
1 small zucchini, diced
¾ cup diced kielbasa sausage (about 4 ounces)
4 mushrooms, sliced
¼ cup chopped drained oil-packed sun-dried tomatoes
1 tablespoon chopped fresh basil or 1 teaspoon dried, crumbled
1 tablespoon chopped fresh oregano or 1 teaspoon dried, crumbled

2 small Bobolis (baked cheese pizza crusts) (1 8-ounce package)
¼ cup purchased pizza sauce
¼ cup grated Parmesan cheese
¼ cup grated mozzarella cheese
2 ounces goat cheese, crumbled

Heat oil in heavy large skillet over medium-low heat. Add zucchini, sausage and mushrooms and sauté until vegetables are almost tender, about 5 minutes. Add sun-dried tomatoes and sauté until vegetables are tender, about 3 minutes longer. Remove skillet from heat; stir in basil and oregano.

Preheat oven to 450°F. Arrange pizza shells on small cookie sheet. Spread half of pizza sauce over each. Sprinkle each with half of Parmesan. Divide vegetable mixture between pizzas. Top each with half of mozzarella and half of goat cheese. Bake until mozzarella melts and pizzas are heated through, about 9 minutes. Serve immediately.

Mexican Pizza

Makes 1 10-inch pizza

6 ounces ground beef
½ 1.25-ounce package taco
   seasoning mix

2 10-inch flour tortillas
1¼ cups grated cheddar cheese
1 cup grated Monterey Jack cheese

1 cup chopped tomato
⅓ cup sliced green onions
¼ cup diced pitted green olives
¼ cup diced pitted black olives
1½ tablespoons sliced drained
   pickled jalapeño chilies

Cook beef and taco seasoning in heavy medium skillet over medium heat until beef is brown, crumbling with fork, about 5 minutes. Cool.

Preheat broiler. Heat heavy large skillet over high heat. Add 1 tortilla and cook until crisp, turning occasionally, about 2 minutes. Remove from skillet. Cook second tortilla until crisp, turning occasionally, about 2 minutes. Leave tortilla in skillet and reduce heat to medium. Sprinkle cheddar cheese over tortilla in skillet. Top with second tortilla. Continue cooking until cheese melts, pressing with spatula, about 2 minutes more. Transfer to 12-inch pizza pan. Top with cooked beef, then Jack cheese. Broil until cheese melts, about 3 minutes. Sprinkle tomato; onions, olives and chilies over pizza. Cut into wedges; serve.

❦ *Sandwiches*

Salade Niçoise Sandwiches

Make these ahead; they get better the longer they stand.

6 servings

1 12½-ounce can tuna packed in
   water, well drained
1 6⅛-ounce can tuna packed in
   water, well drained
3 tablespoons drained capers
¼ cup mayonnaise
1½ tablespoons fresh lemon juice
2 1-pound loaves soft French or
   Italian bread

6 tablespoons (about) olive paste
   (olivada) or olive spread*
2 ½-ounce packages fresh arugula
   or watercress
2 tomatoes, sliced
1 red onion, thinly sliced

Combine all tuna, capers, mayonnaise and fresh lemon juice in medium bowl. Season with pepper. Cut each bread loaf crosswise into 3 pieces, then halve each piece lengthwise. Pull out centers of bread pieces, leaving ½-inch-thick crusts. Spread olive paste on inside of each bread piece. Cover olive paste with generous amount of arugula. Spread ½ cup tuna mixture onto each bottom piece of bread. Top with sliced tomato and sliced onion, then with top pieces of bread. Wrap each sandwich tightly in foil. Refrigerate until departing for picnic. (*Can be prepared 6 hours ahead.*)

*An olive spread available at Italian markets and specialty foods stores. If unavailable, use pureed, pitted, brine-cured black olives, such as Kalamata.

BLT & G(uacamole)

Replacing the mayo with guacamole turns the familiar bacon, lettuce and tomato sandwich into something exciting.

Makes 4

2 large ripe avocados, peeled, pitted
2 tablespoons minced fresh cilantro
2 pickled jalapeño chilies, stemmed, minced
2 teaspoons fresh lime juice

12 thick-cut bacon slices

8 whole-grain bread slices
8 thin tomato slices
4 medium romaine lettuce leaves

Preheat broiler. Mash avocados in medium bowl. Stir in cilantro, jalapeños and lime juice. Season with salt and pepper.

Cook bacon in large skillet over medium-high heat until crisp, turning occasionally, about 7 minutes. Drain.

Meanwhile, lightly toast bread slices on 1 side under broiler. Spread guacamole over untoasted side of each slice while still warm. Place 3 bacon slices on each of 4 bread slices. Top with tomatoes, then lettuce. Place remaining 4 bread slices atop lettuce and serve.

Grilled Eggplant and Tomato Sandwiches

2 servings; can be doubled

3 large Japanese eggplants (about 12 ounces), each cut lengthwise into thirds
1/3 cup olive oil
2 large garlic cloves, minced
1/4 cup chopped fresh basil plus 8 large fresh basil leaves
4 1/2-inch-thick diagonal slices country-style bread

1 large tomato, cut into 1/4-inch-thick slices

4 slices (about 4 ounces) Fontina cheese
Fresh basil sprigs

Prepare barbecue (medium-high heat). Sprinkle eggplant slices generously with salt. Let stand 5 minutes. Pat dry. Combine oil, garlic and chopped basil in small bowl. Season with salt and pepper. Brush eggplant slices, bread and tomato slices with garlic oil.

Grill eggplant until very tender and slightly charred, turning frequently, about 7 minutes per side. Arrange bread and tomatoes on barbecue during last 3 minutes of eggplant-grilling time and cook until bread is golden and tomatoes begin to soften, about 1 minute per side.

Transfer 2 bread slices to plate. Top each remaining bread slice on grill with eggplant, cheese, tomato slices and whole basil leaves, dividing evenly. Season with salt and pepper. Cover grill until cheese just melts, about 1 minute. Transfer sandwiches to plates. Top with second bread slices. Garnish with basil sprigs.

Fried Prosciutto and Cheese Sandwiches

Makes 16

8 ½-inch-thick slices egg bread
24 fresh sage leaves
4 ounces Parmesan cheese, very thinly sliced
2 thin prosciutto slices, halved
4 ounces mozzarella cheese, grated

⅔ cup half and half
3 large eggs

2 tablespoons olive oil

Place 4 bread slices on work surface. Arrange 3 sage leaves on each slice. Top with enough Parmesan cheese slices to cover bread in even layer. Season with pepper. Top each with 1 piece of prosciutto, then ¼ of mozzarella cheese. Cover with remaining Parmesan. Arrange 3 sage leaves atop each. Top with remaining bread slices, pressing slightly.

Beat half and half and eggs together in large shallow dish. Add sandwiches and soak 3 minutes per side.

Heat oil in heavy large skillet over medium-low heat. Add sandwiches and cook until golden brown, about 4 minutes. Turn, cover pan and cook sandwiches until cheese begins to melt, about 6 minutes. Cool slightly. Cut sandwiches into quarters and serve.

Pesto Chicken-Cheese Sandwiches

Makes 4

1 large red bell pepper

4 boneless skinless chicken breast halves (about 1½ pounds)
1 cup purchased pesto sauce

2 tablespoons olive oil
2 tablespoons unsalted butter, room temperature
2 garlic cloves, minced
4 large country-style bread slices
½ pound Fontina cheese, sliced

Char pepper over gas flame or under broiler until blackened on all sides. Place pepper in paper bag and cool 10 minutes. Peel and core pepper. Cut into matchstick-size strips. Set aside.

Combine chicken and ½ cup pesto in shallow dish. Marinate 1 hour in refrigerator, turning occasionally.

Heat heavy large skillet over medium heat. Add chicken and cook until light brown and cooked through, about 5 minutes per side. Transfer to work surface; cover with foil and let rest 5 minutes. Cut chicken diagonally into thin slices. Season with salt and pepper.

Preheat broiler. Whisk together oil, butter and garlic in bowl. Season with salt and pepper. Spread mixture evenly over 1 side of each bread slice. Place bread slices, garlic side up, on broilerproof pan. Broil until garlic mixture bubbles and is golden, about 1 minute. Spread remaining ½ cup pesto over bread slices. Top with chicken, then roasted pepper. Divide cheese evenly among sandwiches. Broil until cheese melts, about 3 minutes.

4 ❦ Main Courses

When "What's for dinner?" is the question you're looking to answer, turn to this chapter again and again for terrific ideas for everything from simple, midweek family suppers to formal Saturday night dinner parties. Here you'll find more than sixty recipes for new things to do with beef, veal, lamb, pork, poultry and seafood, plus a number of excellent egg, cheese and vegetable dishes.

Sometimes you just want a steak, and when you do, consider New York Steak with Green Chili Corn Relish and Fried Onions, a classic steak with real southwestern style, or wonderfully rich Steaks with Wild Mushroom Cream Sauce. Beef on the backyard grill was never so interesting as Grilled Beef with Barbecue Rub and "Mop," a tenderloin coated with a spicy rub, basted with a smoky "mop" and served with Ranch Tomato Sauce. For a simple, quick-cooking take on veal, there's Veal with Lemon, Capers and Parsley. If it's lamb you have in mind, Lamb Kebabs with Peanut Sauce are an exotically different, Southeast Asian-flavored idea; and if you're in the mood for pork, Hot and Spicy Pork Vindaloo conjures up the cooking of India.

Poultry is one of the most versatile dinner options, going from simple to sophisticated—such as quick-cooking Garlic-Lime Chicken to restaurant-style Chicken, Black Bean and Goat Cheese Tostadas—with ease. Seafood, too, lends itself to any number of different preparations, from the deliciously straightforward Salmon with Arugula, Tomato and Caper Sauce to the imaginative Whitefish with Spiced Pecans and Roasted Pepper Sauce.

And if you, like a lot of people, are eating a bit lighter these days, you'll find meatless options in the Eggs, Cheese and Vegetables section, including a low-fat rendition of a classic, Vegetable Paella.

❦ Beef

Grilled Beef with Barbecue Rub and "Mop"

10 servings

Spice Rub
- ¼ cup chopped fresh parsley
- 3 tablespoons coarse salt
- 3 tablespoons coarsely ground pepper
- 2 tablespoons minced garlic
- 1 tablespoon paprika
- 2 teaspoons crumbled bay leaf
- 1½ teaspoons cayenne pepper
- 1½ teaspoons dry mustard

Mop
- 1 cup beef stock or canned broth
- ¼ cup dry red wine

- 3 tablespoons purchased barbecue sauce
- 2 tablespoons Worcestershire sauce
- 2 tablespoons vegetable oil
- 2 large garlic cloves, pressed
- 1 tablespoon minced serrano chili*

- 1 3½-pound beef tenderloin
  Vegetable oil

  Ranch Tomato Sauce (see recipe)

For spice rub: Combine all ingredients in small bowl.

For mop: Combine first 7 ingredients in medium bowl. (*Can be prepared 1 day ahead. Cover spice rub and mop separately and refrigerate.*)

Brush beef with oil. Press spice rub onto beef. Let stand 40 minutes.

Prepare barbecue (medium-high heat). Place beef on grill and cook until thermometer registers 125°F for rare, turning and basting with mop every 5 minutes, about 20 minutes. Move beef to coolest part of grill. Cover with foil and cook 10 minutes more. Transfer to platter and let stand 10 minutes. Slice beef and serve with hot Ranch Tomato Sauce.

*A *serrano* is a very hot, small fresh green chili available at Latin American markets and supermarkets.

Ranch Tomato Sauce

Makes about 2½ cups

- 2 tablespoons vegetable oil
- 1 medium red onion, chopped
- 2 large garlic cloves, chopped
- 1¼ pounds tomatoes, peeled, seeded, chopped
- 1 cup canned tomato sauce
- 2 poblano chilies,* seeded, chopped

- 1 tablespoon red wine vinegar
- 1 teaspoon chopped fresh oregano or ½ teaspoon dried, crumbled
- 1 teaspoon chopped fresh basil or ½ teaspoon dried, crumbled

- 2 tablespoons (¼ stick) butter

Heat vegetable oil in heavy large saucepan over medium heat. Add chopped onion and garlic and sauté until soft, about 10 minutes. Add tomatoes, tomato sauce, chilies, vinegar, oregano and basil and cook until slightly thickened, stirring occasionally, about 10 minutes. Season to taste with salt and pepper. (*Can be made 1 day ahead. Cover and refrigerate. Reheat before continuing.*)

Whisk butter into sauce and serve immediately.

*A *poblano* is a fresh green chili, sometimes called a fresh *pasilla*, available at Latin American markets and also at some supermarkets.

New York Steak with Green Chili Corn Relish and Fried Onions

A classic steak with south-western style.

6 servings

Relish
- 8 ounces Anaheim chilies*
- 2 ears corn or 2 cups frozen kernels, thawed
- 1 teaspoon olive oil
- ¼ red onion, chopped
- 3 garlic cloves, chopped
- 1 tomato, peeled, seeded, chopped
- 1 bunch fresh cilantro, chopped

Onions
- Vegetable oil (for deep frying)
- 1 cup all purpose flour
- 3 large onions, thinly sliced
- Cayenne pepper

Steaks
- 6 8-ounce New York steaks
- Olive oil

For relish: Preheat broiler. Place Anaheim chilies on cookie sheet. Broil until slightly charred, turning often. Wrap in plastic bag and cool. Peel skin from chilies. Remove stems and seeds; dice chilies. Transfer to bowl and set aside.

Cook corn ears or kernels in large pot of boiling water 3 minutes. Drain and cool. Cut kernels off cobs. Add to chilies. (*Chili-corn mixture can be prepared 1 day ahead. Cover and refrigerate.*)

Heat 1 teaspoon olive oil in heavy small skillet over medium heat. Add chopped onion and garlic. Sauté until onion is translucent, about 6 minutes. Mix in chili-corn mixture and chopped tomato and cook 2 minutes. Remove from heat. Stir in cilantro. Season to taste with salt and pepper.

For onions: Heat vegetable oil in deep pot to 375°F. Place flour in large bowl. Dredge sliced onions in flour, shaking off excess. Deep-fry onions in batches until golden brown, about 3 minutes. Using slotted spoon, transfer onions to paper towels and drain. Season to taste with salt and cayenne.

Meanwhile, prepare steaks: Rub steaks lightly with oil. Season with salt and pepper. Heat heavy large skillet over high heat. Add steaks and cook about 4 minutes per side for medium-rare. Transfer steaks to plates.

Top steaks with relish and fried onions and serve.

*Available at Latin American markets and specialty foods stores.

Calf's Liver with Port Wine Sauce

This rich, elegant dish makes a fine entrée for a special occasion.

2 servings

- 4 bacon slices
- ⅓ cup all purpose flour
- 1 teaspoon salt
- ¼ teaspoon pepper
- ⅛ teaspoon ground dried thyme
- 12 ounces sliced calf's liver
- 1 small onion, chopped
- ¼ cup canned beef broth
- ¼ cup Port
- 2 tablespoons red wine vinegar

Cook bacon in heavy large skillet over medium-high heat until crisp. Transfer bacon to paper towel to drain. Discard all but 2 tablespoons fat from pan. Crumble bacon. Set aside.

Combine flour, salt, pepper and thyme in shallow dish. Add liver and turn to coat; shake off excess. Heat fat in skillet over medium-high heat. Add liver and cook until tender and brown on both sides, about 5 minutes. Transfer liver to plate; cover with foil and keep warm. Add onion to skillet and sauté until golden, about 5 minutes. Mix in broth, Port and vinegar. Boil mixture until reduced to sauce, about 2 minutes. Season to taste with salt and pepper. Pour sauce over liver. Sprinkle with bacon and serve.

Filet Mignon with Red Wine Sauce

6 servings

3 cups dry red wine
3 tablespoons Cognac
3 shallots, chopped
1 teaspoon chopped fresh thyme
 or 1 teaspoon dried, crumbled
6 6-ounce filet mignon steaks

4 cups beef stock or canned
 unsalted broth

4 tablespoons olive oil
5 tablespoons chilled unsalted
 butter, cut into pieces

Whisk first 4 ingredients in large bowl. Divide steaks between 2 glass baking dishes. Pour marinade over. Cover and refrigerate overnight.

Remove steaks from marinade and pat dry. Transfer marinade to heavy large saucepan. Boil until reduced to 1 cup, about 20 minutes. Add stock and boil until reduced to 1¼ cups, about 20 minutes. Set aside. (*Can be prepared 4 hours ahead. Cover and refrigerate steaks and sauce separately. Bring steaks to room temperature before continuing.*)

Divide oil between 2 heavy large skillets and place over high heat. Season steaks with salt and pepper. Add 3 steaks to each skillet and brown on both sides. Reduce heat to medium-high and cook to desired doneness, about 4 minutes per side for medium-rare. Transfer steaks to plates. Tent with foil to keep warm. Add half of sauce to each skillet and bring to boil, scraping up any browned bits. Transfer contents of both skillets to 1 skillet and bring to simmer. Add butter and whisk until melted. Spoon sauce over steaks and serve.

Prime Rib Steaks with White Beans and Black Olive Puree

4 servings

Beans
1¼ cups dried cannellini, Great
 Northern or other white beans

1 tablespoon olive oil
½ medium onion, chopped
4 garlic cloves, minced
1 tablespoon chopped fresh
 rosemary or 1 teaspoon dried,
 crumbled
1 tablespoon chopped fresh thyme
 or 1 teaspoon dried, crumbled
5 cups chicken stock or canned
 low-salt broth
1 cup water
1 smoked ham hock

2 tablespoons balsamic vinegar
 or red wine vinegar
1 bay leaf

Sauce
1 tablespoon butter
3 shallots, chopped
1 tablespoon cracked pepper
½ cup dry red wine
½ cup Port
2 cups chicken stock or canned
 low-salt broth
1 cup beef stock or canned
 unsalted broth

4 1-inch-thick rib-eye steaks
¼ cup olivada*

For beans: Place beans in pot. Add enough cold water to cover by 3 inches and let soak overnight. Drain beans.

Heat oil in heavy large saucepan over medium heat. Add onion, garlic and herbs and sauté until onion is translucent, about 8 minutes. Add beans and toss to coat. Add chicken stock, 1 cup water, ham hock, vinegar and bay leaf and bring to boil. Reduce heat, cover and simmer until beans are tender, stirring occasionally, about 2 hours. Season with salt and pepper. (*Can be made 1 day ahead. Cover and refrigerate.*)

For sauce: Melt butter in heavy medium skillet over medium heat. Add shallots and pepper and cook until shallots are translucent, stirring occasionally, about 3 minutes. Add red wine and Port and boil until almost reduced to glaze, about 3 minutes. Add stocks and boil until reduced to 1 cup, about 20 minutes. Season with salt and pepper. (*Can be made 1 day ahead. Cover and chill.*)

Prepare barbecue (medium-high heat). Season steaks with salt and pepper. Grill to desired doneness, about 4 minutes per side for rare. Transfer steaks to plates. Spread 1 tablespoon olivada over each. Tent with foil.

Bring beans and sauce to simmer, stirring frequently. Spoon beans around steaks. Spoon sauce over steaks and serve.

*An olive spread available at Italian markets and specialty foods stores. If unavailable, use pureed, pitted, brine-cured black olives, such as Kalamata.

Beef Paprikás

6 servings

4 tablespoons (½ stick) (about) unsalted butter
2 large onions, chopped
1 large green bell pepper, chopped
1 pound mushrooms, sliced
2 tablespoons all purpose flour
1½ tablespoons paprika (preferably Hungarian sweet)
2½ cups beef stock or canned unsalted broth

1 tablespoon tomato paste
¾ cup sour cream
3 tablespoons chopped fresh dill

1¾ pounds center-cut beef tenderloin (chateaubriand), cut into ¼- to ½-inch-thick slices, slices halved lengthwise
¼ cup dry white wine
Chopped tomatoes (optional)

Melt 2 tablespoons butter in heavy large deep skillet over medium heat. Add onions and bell pepper and sauté until light golden, about 10 minutes. Add mushrooms and sauté until starting to soften, about 5 minutes. Mix in flour and paprika and stir 2 minutes. Mix in stock and tomato paste. Bring to boil, stirring constantly. Boil until sauce thickens and paprika flavor mellows, stirring frequently, about 8 minutes. Mix in sour cream. Remove from heat and add dill. Season to taste with salt and pepper. (*Can be prepared 1 day ahead. Cover and refrigerate. Bring to simmer before adding beef.*)

Melt 1 tablespoon butter in another heavy large skillet over medium-high heat. Working in batches, add beef, season with salt and pepper and cook until just brown on each side. Transfer to plate. Add more butter as needed. When all beef is brown, add to sauce along with any drippings on plate. Add dry white wine to skillet and bring to boil, scraping up any browned bits. Boil until syrupy, about 3 minutes. Add wine to beef. Sprinkle dish with chopped tomatoes before serving, if desired.

Steaks with Wild Mushroom Cream Sauce

2 servings

2 tablespoons olive oil
1 large shallot, minced
½ cup brandy
2 cups unsalted beef stock
½ cup whipping cream

½ pound fresh wild mushrooms (such as chanterelle, morel or oyster) or button mushrooms, sliced

1 tablespoon butter
2 8-ounce beef sirloin steaks (about ¾ inch thick)

Heat 1 tablespoon olive oil in heavy large skillet over medium heat. Add minced shallot and sauté 3 minutes. Remove skillet from heat. Add brandy and ignite with match. When flames subside, return skillet to heat. Add unsalted beef stock and boil until reduced to ½ cup, stirring occasionally, about 15 minutes. Add whipping cream and bring to boil. (*Sauce can be prepared 1 day ahead. Cover and refrigerate. Bring to simmer before continuing.*)

Stir mushrooms into sauce. Reduce heat and simmer until tender, stirring occasionally, about 20 minutes. Season to taste with salt and pepper.

Melt butter with remaining 1 tablespoon oil in heavy medium skillet over high heat. Add steaks and brown on both sides, about 2 minutes. Reduce heat to medium and cook to desired doneness, about 3 minutes per side for medium-rare. Transfer steaks to plates. Add mushroom sauce to beef cooking skillet and bring to simmer, scraping up browned bits. Spoon sauce over steaks.

Spencer Steaks with Shiitake Sauce

4 servings

10 tablespoons (1¼ sticks) butter
12 ounces fresh shiitake mushrooms, stemmed, sliced
⅓ cup minced shallots
1½ cups dry red wine
3¼ cups canned unsalted beef broth
4 fresh thyme sprigs

2 tablespoons minced fresh thyme
2 teaspoons light soy sauce

4 6- to 8-ounce Spencer (boneless rib-eye) steaks
1 tablespoon vegetable oil

Chopped fresh thyme
Fresh thyme sprigs

Melt 4 tablespoons butter in heavy large skillet over medium-high heat. Add mushrooms and shallots and sauté until tender, about 4 minutes. Add ¾ cup wine and boil until reduced to glaze, about 4 minutes. Add remaining ¾ cup wine and boil until reduced to glaze, about 4 minutes. Add 3 cups broth and 4 thyme sprigs and boil until syrupy, about 20 minutes. Add minced thyme and soy sauce. (*Can be made 2 hours ahead. Cover and let stand at room temperature.*)

Cover steaks with generous amount of ground pepper. Melt 2 tablespoons butter with oil in heavy large skillet over high heat. Add steaks and brown on each side. Reduce heat to medium and cook steaks to designed doneness. Transfer to heated plates and keep warm.

Pour off drippings from skillet. Add remaining ¼ cup broth and bring to boil, scraping up any browned bits. Boil until syrupy, about 1 minute. Add to sauce. Bring to simmer. Whisk in 4 tablespoons butter. Season with salt and pepper. Discard thyme sprigs from sauce and spoon sauce over steaks. Sprinkle with chopped thyme. Garnish with thyme sprigs.

❦ Veal

Veal with Blue Cheese Sauce

This is a Spanish dish. In Spain it would be made with Tresviso-Picón, one of the country's great blue-veined cheeses. Since you probably won't find it at your local market, use any good-quality domestic or imported blue cheese.

4 servings

3 tablespoons unsalted butter
1 cup shelled fresh peas or frozen
½ pound mushrooms, quartered
¼ cup brandy
1 cup whipping cream

1 cup crumbled blue cheese (about 5 ounces)

4 8-ounce ½-inch-thick veal loin chops

Melt 2 tablespoons butter in heavy large skillet over medium-high heat. Add peas and mushrooms and sauté 5 minutes. Transfer vegetables to bowl using slotted spoon. Add brandy to same skillet and bring to boil. Add cream and cheese to skillet and boil until reduced to sauce consistency, stirring occasionally, about 8 minutes. (*Can be prepared 2 hours ahead. Cover vegetables and sauce separately and let stand at room temperature.*)

Melt remaining 1 tablespoon butter in another heavy large skillet over medium-high heat. Season veal chops with salt and pepper. Add veal to skillet and cook to desired doneness, about 3 minutes per side for medium. Transfer veal to plates. Add vegetables to veal cooking skillet and heat through. Bring sauce to simmer. Spoon over veal. Garnish with vegetables and serve.

Veal Stew with Mushrooms and Peppers

4 servings

4 tablespoons olive oil
1 pound veal stew meat, cut into 1-inch cubes
   All purpose flour
12 large mushrooms, quartered
1 large red bell pepper, sliced
1 tablespoon dried oregano, crumbled

½ teaspoon ground allspice
¼ teaspoon dried crushed red pepper
¾ cup dry Marsala
3 large garlic cloves, minced
½ cup low-salt chicken broth

   Steamed white rice

Preheat oven to 350°F. Heat 2 tablespoons oil in heavy large ovenproof skillet over medium-high heat. Dredge veal in flour, shaking off excess. Add veal to skillet and cook until brown, stirring occasionally, about 5 minutes. Transfer veal to plate using slotted spoon. Heat remaining 2 tablespoons oil in same skillet. Add mushrooms, bell pepper, oregano, allspice and crushed red pepper to skillet. Sauté until mushrooms are just beginning to brown, about 3 minutes. Stir in Marsala and garlic and boil until skillet is almost dry, about 4 minutes. Add veal and any juices accumulated on plate to skillet. Mix in chicken broth and bring to boil. Cover and bake in oven until veal is very tender, about 1 hour. (*Can be prepared 1 day ahead. Cover and refrigerate.*)

Transfer stew to stove and boil until liquid thickens to sauce consistency, about 12 minutes. Serve with rice.

Veal with Braised Fennel, Tomato Confit and Wild Mushrooms

4 servings

Confit
- ¼ cup plus 2 tablespoons olive oil
- ⅔ cup finely chopped onion
- 1 small bay leaf
- 1 fresh thyme sprig or ½ teaspoon dried, crumbled
- 2 tomatoes, peeled, seeded, chopped

Mushrooms
- 1 tablespoon butter
- 8 ounces chanterelles or other wild mushrooms
- ⅓ cup water

Veal
- 7 tablespoons butter
- 4 1½-inch-thick veal chops
- 2 tablespoons water

- ¼ cup whipping cream
- 2 tablespoons chopped fresh chives
- 2 teaspoons fresh lemon juice
  Braised Fennel (see recipe)

For confit: Heat oil in heavy medium skillet over low heat. Add onion, bay leaf and thyme sprig and sauté until onion is tender, about 8 minutes; do not brown. Add tomatoes and cook until jamlike and no liquid remains, stirring occasionally, approximately 20 minutes.

For mushrooms: Melt butter in heavy large skillet over medium-high heat. Add mushrooms. Cover and cook 2 minutes. Add water and cook until liquid evaporates, stirring occasionally, about 6 minutes. Season to taste with salt and pepper. (*Confit and mushrooms can be prepared 2 hours ahead. Cover separately; let stand at room temperature.*)

For veal: Melt 2 tablespoons butter in heavy large skillet over low heat. Season veal with salt and pepper. Add to skillet and sauté until just cooked through, about 8 minutes per side. Transfer to plates and keep warm. Stir water into skillet and bring to boil, scraping up any browned bits. Pour over veal.

Add cream to mushrooms and bring to boil over medium heat. Mix in remaining 5 tablespoons butter. Stir in chives and lemon juice. Season with salt and pepper. Reheat tomatoes over low heat until just warm. Remove bay leaf and thyme sprig. Arrange mushrooms, tomato confit and Braised Fennel around veal and serve immediately.

Braised Fennel

Nice with any roast meat.

4 servings

- 3 tablespoons butter
- ¼ cup chopped shallots
  Seeds from 2 cardamom pods, crushed
- ⅛ teaspoon ground mace
- 2 medium fennel bulbs, each cut lengthwise into 6 pieces
- 1¼ cups chicken stock

Preheat oven to 350°F. Melt butter in heavy medium ovenproof skillet over low heat. Add shallots, cardamom and mace and sauté 8 minutes. Add fennel and toss to coat. Stir in stock and bring to boil. Cover and braise in oven 30 minutes, basting occasionally. Remove skillet from oven. Place on burner over high heat and boil until liquid thickens slightly, 15 minutes. Season with salt and pepper.

Veal with Lemon, Capers and Parsley

2 servings

6 ounces veal scallops
All purpose flour
2 tablespoons olive oil
3 tablespoons unsalted butter

2 tablespoons fresh lemon juice
2 tablespoons chopped fresh
   parsley
1 tablespoon drained capers

Season veal with salt and pepper. Coat with flour; shake off excess. Heat oil in heavy large skillet over high heat. Add veal and sauté just until cooked through, about 1 minute per side. Divide veal between plates. Tent with foil to keep warm. Add butter, lemon juice, parsley and capers to same skillet and whisk just until butter melts. Season to taste with salt and pepper. Spoon sauce over veal.

❦ Lamb

Broiled Lamb Chops with Green Peppercorn Sauce

4 servings

Lamb
6 ½-inch-thick lamb shoulder blade
   chops
2 large garlic cloves, halved
1½ tablespoons olive oil
1 tablespoon dried rosemary,
   crumbled

Sauce
2 tablespoons (¼ stick) butter
1 small onion, minced
1 cup sliced mushrooms

1 teaspoon minced fresh thyme or
   ¼ teaspoon dried, crumbled
1 teaspoon minced fresh parsley
½ cup tawny Port
¼ cup canned low-salt chicken
   broth
1 tablespoon drained green
   peppercorns in brine
2 teaspoons Dijon mustard

½ cup crème fraîche or whipping
   cream

For lamb: Rub lamb chops all over with cut side of garlic. Brush all over with oil. Sprinkle both sides of lamb with rosemary. Cover and refrigerate at least 4 hours or overnight.

For sauce: Melt butter in heavy large skillet over medium heat. Add onion and sauté 2 minutes. Add mushrooms, thyme and parsley and sauté 4 minutes. Add Port and boil until reduced by half, about 3 minutes. Add broth, peppercorns and mustard and boil until slightly thickened, stirring occasionally, about 4 minutes. (*Can be prepared 1 day ahead. Cover and chill.*)

Preheat broiler. Broil lamb chops to desired degree of doneness, about 4 minutes per side for medium-rare.

Meanwhile, add crème fraîche to sauce and boil until reduced to sauce consistency, stirring occasionally, about 5 minutes. Season with salt and pepper. Serve lamb immediately with sauce.

Spicy Lamb and Peanut Stew

8 servings

2 tablespoons peanut oil
1¾ pounds lamb shoulder, trimmed, cut into 1-inch cubes
2 large onions, coarsely chopped
1 6-ounce can tomato paste
3 bay leaves
¼ teaspoon cayenne pepper
1¾ cups beef stock or canned broth
1¾ cups water

¾ cup old-fashioned style or freshly ground peanut butter
1 cup diced carrots
4 jalapeño or 2 habañero chilies, halved, seeded
1 cup frozen peas
Freshly cooked rice

Heat oil in heavy large saucepan or Dutch oven over medium-high heat. Add lamb and onions and cook until lamb is brown, stirring occasionally, about 6 minutes. Mix in tomato paste, bay leaves and cayenne pepper and cook 1 minute. Season with salt and pepper. Add beef stock and water and bring to boil. Simmer until lamb is tender, about 1 hour 20 minutes.

Stir peanut butter, carrots and jalapeños into stew and cook until carrots are tender, about 30 minutes. Add peas and cook until heated through. Discard jalapeños. Serve stew over rice.

Grilled Leg of Lamb with Chimichurri Sauce

Chimichurri *is a classic spicy Argentine condiment. In this version, it's both a marinade and a sauce (when serving it as a sauce, use sparingly—it's hot).*

10 servings

2 cups cold water
½ cup olive oil
6 tablespoons dried oregano, crumbled
6 garlic cloves, chopped
1 tablespoon paprika
1 tablespoon salt

1 teaspoon dried crushed red pepper
1 teaspoon pepper
1 teaspoon white pepper

2 4-pound butterflied legs of lamb

Whisk first 9 ingredients in medium bowl. Cover sauce and let stand overnight at room temperature. (*Can be prepared 1 week ahead; refrigerate. Bring sauce to room temperature before using.*)

Place each leg of lamb in separate glass or ceramic (do not use metal) baking dish. Pour ½ cup sauce over each. Reserve remaining sauce. Cover and refrigerate lamb 3 hours.

Prepare barbecue (medium-high heat). Remove lamb from marinade; discard marinade. Grill lamb to desired doneness, about 12 minutes per side for medium-rare. Transfer lamb to work surface. Let stand 10 minutes. Slice lamb diagonally. Transfer to platter. Pass remaining sauce separately.

Lamb Kebabs with Peanut Sauce

Broiling, rather than grill-ing, the kebabs makes this Southeast Asian-flavored dish a year-round winner.

2 servings

3/4 cup canned chicken broth
1/2 cup milk
1 cup creamy peanut butter (do not use old-fashioned style or freshly ground)
2 teaspoons ground cumin
2 teaspoons curry powder
1 to 2 tablespoons fresh lime juice

14 ounces boneless leg of lamb, cut into 12 1 1/2-inch cubes
1 medium onion, cut into 12 pieces
1 small red bell pepper, cut into 12 squares
4 12-inch-long wooden skewers, soaked in water 30 minutes
Freshly cooked rice

Bring broth and milk to simmer in heavy small saucepan over medium heat. Add peanut butter and stir until smooth and heated through. Mix in cumin, curry powder and lime juice to taste. Season with salt and pepper. Remove from heat.

Preheat broiler. Alternate 3 lamb cubes, 3 onion pieces and 3 bell pepper squares on each skewer. Season with salt and pepper. Brush kebabs with peanut sauce. Broil to desired doneness, about 5 minutes per side for medium-rare. Serve kebabs with rice, passing remaining sauce separately.

❦ Pork

Roast Pork Calypso Style

Slices of cold roast pork and avocado fanned around a black bean salad are drizzled with an orange sauce in this dish.

4 servings

3 shallots, chopped
2 bay leaves, crumbled
1 1/2 teaspoons salt
3/4 teaspoon ground allspice
3/4 teaspoon ground ginger
2 3/4-pound pork tenderloins

Sauce
1 1/2 cups orange juice
1/4 cup minced shallots
3 tablespoons brown sugar

2 tablespoons minced peeled fresh ginger
2 bay leaves
3/8 teaspoon ground allspice

Fresh spinach leaves
Salad of Black Beans, Hearts of Palm and Corn (see recipe)
2 avocados, peeled, pitted, sliced crosswise
Minced fresh parsley

Preheat oven to 450°F. Combine shallots, bay leaves, salt, allspice and ginger in small bowl. Add generous amount of pepper. Rub mixture into pork. Set on rack in roasting pan. Roast pork until thermometer inserted into centers registers 150°F, about 25 minutes. Cool slightly. (*Can be prepared 1 day ahead. Refrigerate. Bring pork to room temperature before serving.*)

For sauce: Combine first 6 ingredients in heavy small saucepan. Season with pepper. Simmer until slightly syrupy, about 10 minutes. (*Can be prepared 1 day ahead. Cover and refrigerate.*)

Line platter with spinach. Mound black bean salad in center. Slice pork. Alternate pork and avocado slices around salad. Discard bay leaves from sauce and drizzle sauce over pork and avocado. Sprinkle with parsley.

Salad of Black Beans, Hearts of Palm and Corn

4 servings

1 16-ounce can black beans, rinsed, drained
1 10-ounce package frozen corn, thawed, drained
1 7½-ounce can hearts of palm, drained, cut into ¼-inch-thick rounds

2 large tomatoes, seeded, diced
½ red onion, minced
½ cup chopped fresh cilantro
¼ cup olive oil
3 tablespoons fresh lime juice
1 teaspoon ground coriander

Mix all ingredients in medium bowl. Season salad to taste with salt and pepper. (*Salad can be prepared 1 day ahead. Cover and refrigerate.*)

Lemon- and Soy-marinated Pork Tenderloins

8 servings

¾ cup fresh lemon juice
½ cup soy sauce
6 tablespoons honey
2 small shallots, coarsely chopped
2 large garlic cloves, halved
2 bay leaves, crumbled

2 teaspoons salt
2 teaspoons pepper
1 teaspoon dry mustard
½ teaspoon ground ginger
4 12-ounce pork tenderloins

Puree first 10 ingredients in blender. Divide pork tenderloins between 2 large resealable plastic bags. Add half of marinade to each and seal tightly. Turn to coat. Refrigerate pork overnight.

Prepare barbecue (medium-high heat). Remove pork from marinade. Transfer marinade to heavy saucepan. Grill pork to desired doneness, turning often, about 20 minutes for medium.

Meanwhile, boil marinade in small saucepan until reduced to sauce consistency, approximately 5 minutes.

Slice pork. Serve immediately with sauce.

Orange and Rosemary Pork

Orange juice adds a hint of sweetness to this elegant main course.

6 servings

1 cup orange juice
⅓ cup soy sauce
¼ cup olive oil

2 tablespoons chopped fresh rosemary or 2 teaspoons dried, crumbled
3 garlic cloves, pressed
2 12-ounce pork tenderloins

Combine first 5 ingredients in baking dish. Add pork and marinate in refrigerator at least 1 hour or overnight.

Preheat oven to 400°F. Drain pork, reserving marinade. Place pork on baking sheet and season generously with pepper. Roast pork until cooked through, approximately 20 minutes.

Meanwhile, bring reserved marinade to boil in small saucepan. Slice pork tenderloins and serve, passing marinade separately as sauce.

Pork Loin with Port and Leek Sauce

4 servings

2 cups chicken stock or canned low-salt broth
1 cup beef stock or canned unsalted broth

1½ pounds russet potatoes, peeled, cut into 1-inch pieces
½ cup (1 stick) butter
½ cup whipping cream
Pinch of ground nutmeg

1 tablespoon olive oil
1 pound boneless pork loin

1 large leek (white and pale green parts only), sliced
3 shallots, finely chopped
1 cup Port

Boil both stocks in medium saucepan until reduced to ⅔ cup, about 25 minutes.

Cook potatoes in large saucepan of boiling salted water until tender. Drain. Return to pan and mash with potato masher. Add butter and cream and bring to simmer, stirring frequently. Season to taste with salt, pepper and nutmeg. (*Can be prepared 2 hours ahead. Cover stock mixture and potatoes separately and let stand at room temperature.*)

Preheat oven to 425°F. Heat oil in heavy large ovenproof skillet over high heat. Season pork with salt and pepper. Add to skillet and brown on all sides, about 5 minutes. Transfer skillet to oven and roast pork just until cooked through, about 20 minutes. Transfer pork to plate and tent with foil to keep warm; do not clean skillet.

Add leek and shallots to same skillet and cook over medium heat until tender, about 8 minutes. Add reduced stock mixture and Port and boil until reduced by half, about 4 minutes.

Meanwhile, rewarm mashed potatoes in saucepan over medium heat, stirring frequently. Divide among plates. Cut pork into slices and arrange around potatoes. Spoon Port sauce over pork.

Hot and Spicy Pork Vindaloo

4 servings

¾ cup white wine vinegar
8 whole cloves
8 whole peppercorns
5 garlic cloves
2 tablespoons coriander seeds
1 tablespoon cumin seeds
1 tablespoon mustard seeds
1 tablespoon chili powder
½ teaspoon cardamom seeds (from about 12 pods)

½ teaspoon ground cinnamon
½ teaspoon ground ginger
¼ teaspoon cayenne pepper
1½ pounds boneless country-style pork spareribs, cut into 1½-inch cubes

¼ cup water
Freshly cooked rice

Puree first 12 ingredients in blender until smooth. Place pork in large bowl. Add spice mixture from blender and mix to coat. Cover and marinate in refrigerator at least 3 hours. (*Can be prepared 1 day ahead. Chill.*)

Place pork mixture in large pot or Dutch oven. Add ¼ cup water. Bring to simmer. Reduce heat, cover and simmer until pork is tender, stirring occasionally, about 1 hour 30 minutes. Uncover pot. Simmer pork until liquid thickens to sauce consistency, about 15 minutes. Mound rice on platter. Spoon pork over rice and serve immediately.

Wine-braised Pork Loin

Start marinating the pork at least seven hours ahead. Offer sautéed kale alongside.

6 servings

2 teaspoons salt
½ teaspoon pepper
1 bay leaf, crumbled
1 garlic clove, minced
  Pinch of ground allspice
1 2-pound boned center-cut pork loin roast, rolled, tied

3 tablespoons olive oil
2 onions, chopped

4 garlic cloves, chopped
2 red bell peppers, cut lengthwise into strips, halved crosswise
1 cup dry white wine
1 cup canned crushed tomatoes with added puree
1 cup canned beef broth
2 bay leaves
1 tablespoon dried marjoram, crumbled

Combine first 5 ingredients in small bowl. Pat pork dry; rub with salt mixture. Cover and chill 6 to 24 hours.

Preheat oven to 350°F. Wipe pork dry. Heat 2 tablespoons oil in heavy Dutch oven or casserole over high heat. Add pork; brown on all sides, about 10 minutes. Transfer to plate. Reduce heat to medium and add remaining 1 tablespoon oil to Dutch oven. Add onions and sauté until very tender, about 10 minutes. Add garlic and peppers and sauté until peppers begin to soften, about 5 minutes. Add wine, tomatoes, broth, bay leaves and marjoram. Add pork, fat side up, and drippings on plate. Bring to boil. Cover pork and bake until tender, approximately 45 minutes.

Transfer pork to platter and let stand 15 minutes. If necessary, boil sauce until reduced to 4 cups. Season with salt and pepper. Slice pork. (*Can be prepared 1 day ahead. Place half of sauce in baking dish. Top with pork slices, then remaining sauce. Cover and chill. Rewarm in covered dish in 350°F oven until heated through, about 30 minutes.*) Serve pork with sauce.

Hoisin-glazed Baby Back Ribs

6 servings

1 cup catsup
¾ cup hoisin sauce*
½ cup honey
5 tablespoons soy sauce
5 tablespoons dry Sherry
¼ cup plus 2 teaspoons white wine vinegar
¼ cup sesame seeds
2 tablespoons plus 2 teaspoons curry powder

2 tablespoons plus 2 teaspoons oriental sesame oil
2 tablespoons grated orange peel
2 tablespoons salted black beans,* minced
2 tablespoons minced garlic
1 tablespoon chili paste with garlic*
3 pounds pork baby back ribs

Whisk all ingredients except ribs in large bowl to blend. Divide ribs between 2 large baking dishes. Brush with half of sauce. Cover ribs and remaining sauce separately and refrigerate overnight.

Preheat oven to 375°F. Transfer ribs to heavy large baking sheets. Roast ribs until tender, basting frequently with some of remaining sauce, about 1 hour. Place remaining sauce in heavy small saucepan and bring to simmer. Transfer ribs to platter. Cut into individual ribs. Pass remaining sauce separately.

*Available at Asian markets and at some supermarkets.

Kielbasa Sausage with Spiced Sauerkraut

For a cozy supper, accompany this quickly prepared dish with pumpernickel bread and hot mustard.

4 servings

1 large onion, diced
1 16-ounce can sauerkraut
1 cup dry white wine
2 bay leaves

½ teaspoon caraway seeds
6 peppercorns
1 pound kielbasa sausage, sliced

Combine onion, sauerkraut, wine, bay leaves, caraway seeds and peppercorns in heavy large saucepan. Cover and simmer mixture 30 minutes. Add sausage and simmer 20 minutes. Discard bay leaves and serve.

❦ Poultry and Game

Roast Pheasant with Apples

This simple roast recipe is from Rathsallagh House, a country home in Dunlavin, County Wicklow, near the town of Dublin.

4 servings

2 tablespoons (¼ stick) unsalted butter
1½ cups chopped unpeeled cored apple
1 cup chopped onion
4 juniper berries, crushed, or 1 tablespoon gin

1 3- to 3¾-pound pheasant

1 fresh thyme sprig or pinch of dried, crumbled
¾ cup dry red wine
¾ cup chicken stock or canned low-salt broth

Fresh thyme sprigs (optional)

Melt 1 tablespoon butter in heavy large skillet over medium-low heat. Add apple and onion and sauté until onion is golden and tender, about 8 minutes. Stir in juniper berries. Season with salt and pepper. Cool mixture completely.

Preheat oven to 375°F. Rinse pheasant thoroughly. Pat dry. Pull off any pinfeathers and discard any clumps of fat. Season pheasant inside and out with salt and pepper. Spoon apple-onion stuffing into cavity; add 1 thyme sprig. Close cavity with metal skewers.

Melt remaining 1 tablespoon butter in same skillet over medium-low heat. Add pheasant to skillet and cook until light brown on all sides, turning carefully, about 10 minutes. Arrange pheasant on its side in roasting pan. Roast 15 minutes. Turn pheasant onto second side, baste with pan juices and roast 15 minutes longer, basting once. Turn pheasant breast side up and baste with pan juices. Continue roasting until juices run clear when thickest part of thigh is pierced with tip of knife, basting occasionally, about 25 minutes. Transfer pheasant to carving board; tent with aluminum foil to keep warm.

Pour off fat from pan, reserving juices. Boil wine in heavy small saucepan until reduced to ¼ cup, about 4 minutes. Add chicken stock and reserved roasting juices and boil until reduced to ¾ cup, about 8 minutes. Season sauce to taste with salt and pepper.

Remove skin from pheasant and discard. Carve legs from pheasant; cut breast into thick slices. Spoon stuffing onto platter. Arrange pheasant pieces atop stuffing. Drizzle with sauce. Garnish with thyme sprigs if desired.

Chicken, Shrimp and Beef Satés with Peanut Sauce

8 servings

1 cup teriyaki sauce
4 garlic cloves, minced
3 tablespoons fresh lime juice
2½ tablespoons minced fresh ginger
2 tablespoons brown sugar
24 medium uncooked shrimp, peeled, deveined
1¼ pounds boneless skinless chicken breasts, cut into ½-inch-wide strips
1¼ pounds beef skirt steak, cut into 3 × ½-inch strips, or filet mignon, cut into 3 × ½ × ¼-inch strips

36 (about) bamboo skewers, soaked in water 30 minutes

Banana leaves or ornamental kale
Peanut Sauce (see recipe)
Lime slices
Hibiscus or gardenia flowers (optional)

Combine first 5 ingredients in large glass baking dish. Stir until sugar dissolves. Add shrimp, chicken and beef; stir to coat. Cover; chill 30 minutes to 1 hour.

Remove shrimp, chicken and beef from marinade. Thread on separate skewers, using about 3 shrimp per skewer and 2 beef or chicken pieces per skewer. Place on platter. (*Can be prepared 2 hours ahead. Cover and chill.*)

Prepare barbecue (medium-high heat) or preheat broiler. Grill skewered meats until cooked through, about 3 minutes per side. Line large platter with banana leaves. Place sauce in bowl in center of platter. Surround with skewers. Garnish with lime and flowers, if desired, and serve.

Peanut Sauce

Also delicious over pasta or pork.

Makes about 3 cups

1 cup creamy peanut butter (do not use old-fashioned style or freshly ground)
1 14½-ounce can chicken broth
¼ cup fresh lime juice
3 tablespoons brown sugar
2 tablespoons plus 1 teaspoon soy sauce

2 tablespoons chopped peeled fresh ginger
½ teaspoon dried crushed red pepper
Lime peel, cut into matchstick-size strips

Place peanut butter in heavy medium saucepan. Gradually mix in chicken broth. Add all remaining ingredients except lime peel. Stir over medium heat until smooth and thick, about 6 minutes. (*Can be prepared 3 days ahead. Cover and refrigerate. Before serving, stir over medium heat until hot, thinning with water if necessary.*) Pour sauce into bowl and garnish with lime peel.

Chicken Pot Pies

This recipe comes from Chasen's, the fabled Hollywood hangout where the entertainment industry has been dining and dealing for more than 55 years.

10 servings

Filling

18 cups water
 5 2³/₄-pound chickens, quartered
 6 carrots, coarsely chopped
 6 celery stalks, coarsely chopped
 3 small onions, coarsely chopped
 2 bouquet garni (2 bay leaves, 2 thyme sprigs, 2 parsley sprigs and 9 whole black peppercorns, tied up in cheesecloth, for each bouquet)

40 pearl onions
 3 medium carrots, peeled, cut into matchstick-size strips
 3 medium russet potatoes, peeled, cut into 1-inch cubes
2½ cups frozen peas, thawed

Sauce

 1 cup plus 2 tablespoons (2¼ sticks) butter
 3 medium onions, sliced
12 whole peppercorns
 1 cup all purpose flour
1²/₃ cups whipping cream
2½ tablespoons fresh lemon juice
¼ teaspoon hot pepper sauce (such as Tabasco)

Pot Pie Dough (see recipe)

 5 egg yolks, beaten to blend (glaze)

For filling: Divide first 6 ingredients between 2 large pots and bring to boil. Reduce heat and simmer until chicken is tender, about 35 minutes. Using tongs, transfer chicken to large bowl and cool. Strain cooking liquid and return to 1 large pot. Remove skin from chicken. Pull meat from bones in large pieces. Cover chicken meat and refrigerate.

Bring strained cooking liquid to boil. Add pearl onions and blanch 1 minute. Transfer to medium bowl of ice water using slotted spoon and cool. Drain onions. Add carrots to pot and boil until crisp-tender, about 2 minutes. Transfer to medium bowl of ice water using slotted spoon and cool. Drain carrots. Add potatoes to pot and boil until almost tender, about 15 minutes. Transfer potatoes to large bowl using slotted spoon and cool. Reserve 5⅓ cups cooking liquid. Peel pearl onions. Add chicken, onions, carrots and peas to potatoes. (*Filling can be prepared 1 day ahead. Cover and refrigerate.*)

For sauce: Melt 1 cup butter in heavy large saucepan over medium heat. Add sliced onions and whole peppercorns and sauté 5 minutes. Whisk in flour. Cook 2 minutes, whisking constantly. Gradually whisk in 5⅓ cups reserved cooking liquid and whipping cream. Boil 3 minutes, whisking constantly. Mix in fresh lemon juice, hot pepper sauce and remaining 2 tablespoons butter. Season sauce to taste with salt and pepper. Strain sauce. (*Sauce can be prepared 1 day ahead. Cover tightly and refrigerate.*)

Bring sauce to simmer, whisking frequently. Divide chicken and vegetables among ten 3- to 4-cup soufflé dishes or soup crocks (about 6 inches in diameter). Top with sauce. Cool.

Cut each dough disk into 4 pieces. Roll out 1 piece on lightly floured surface to 9-inch round. Place dough round atop soufflé dish, covering completely and trimming dough overhang to 1 inch if necessary. Press dough firmly to sides of soufflé dish to secure. Repeat with remaining dough pieces and soufflé dishes, reserving remaining 2 dough pieces for another use. (*Pies can be prepared 8 hours ahead. Cover and refrigerate. Let stand 30 minutes at room temperature before continuing.*)

Preheat oven to 400°F. Brush egg glaze over dough. Bake chicken pot pies until pastry is deep golden brown, about 30 minutes.

Pot Pie Dough

This dough makes enough to cover ten 3- to 4-cup 6-inch-diameter soufflé dishes, with a little left over. For best results, make the pastry in three batches.

9 cups all purpose flour
3 teaspoons salt

2¼ cups (4½ sticks) chilled unsalted butter, cut into pieces
2¼ cups ice water

Combine 3 cups flour and 1 teaspoon salt in processor. Add ¾ cup (1½ sticks) unsalted butter and cut in using on/off turns until mixture resembles coarse meal. Add ¾ cup ice water and mix in using on/off turns until dough forms moist clumps. Gather dough into ball; flatten into disk. Wrap tightly in plastic and refrigerate. Repeat with remaining flour, salt, butter and ice water in 2 more batches. Refrigerate dough at least 30 minutes. (*Can be prepared 1 day ahead; keep dough refrigerated.*)

Chicken, Black Bean and Goat Cheese Tostadas

6 servings

Beans
2 tablespoons olive oil
1 red onion, chopped
2 large jalapeño chilies, seeded but not deveined, minced
1 teaspoon chili powder
½ teaspoon ground cumin
2 16-ounce cans black beans, rinsed, drained
2 tablespoons fresh lime juice

Chicken
2 tablespoons olive oil
1½ pounds boneless chicken breasts, skinned, cut into ¾-inch pieces
1½ teaspoons chili powder
¾ teaspoon ground cumin

Salad
4 cups sliced romaine lettuce
1 medium head radicchio, sliced
½ cup fresh cilantro leaves

Vegetable oil
6 corn tortillas

¼ cup olive oil
1 tablespoon fresh lime juice
2 tablespoons (about) water
½ pound goat cheese, crumbled
Avocado Salsa (see recipe)
6 fresh cilantro sprigs

For beans: Heat olive oil in heavy medium saucepan over medium-low heat. Add onion and chilies; cook until onion is translucent, stirring occasionally, about 8 minutes. Add chili powder and cumin; stir 30 seconds. Add beans and lime juice. Cook until heated through, stirring and mashing beans slightly with spoon, about 4 minutes. (*Can be prepared 1 day ahead. Cover and chill.*)

For chicken: Heat oil in heavy large skillet over high heat. Add chicken and sprinkle with salt and pepper. Stir until almost cooked through, about 3 minutes. Add chili powder and cumin and stir until cooked through, about 30 seconds. Remove from heat.

For salad: Combine first 3 ingredients in large bowl.

Add oil to depth of ¼ inch to heavy medium skillet. Heat over medium-high heat until just beginning to smoke. Add tortilla and cook until crisp, about 30 seconds per side. Drain on paper towels. Repeat with remaining tortillas.

Add ¼ cup olive oil to salad; toss. Season with salt and pepper. Add 1 tablespoon lime juice; toss. Rewarm beans over medium-low heat, stirring and thinning slightly with water. Place 1 tortilla on each plate. Spread with beans. Sprinkle with cheese. Top with salad, then chicken, salsa and cilantro.

Avocado Salsa

Makes about 4 cups

2 large tomatoes, seeded, diced
½ red onion, chopped
½ cup chopped fresh cilantro
¼ cup olive oil

2 tablespoons fresh lime juice
1 to 2 large jalapeño chilies, seeded
 but not deveined, minced
1 large avocado, diced

Combine first 6 ingredients in medium bowl. Season with salt. (*Can be prepared 2 hours ahead. Cover and refrigerate.*) Add avocado to salsa just before serving.

Roast Venison with Cranberry Compote

4 servings

Venison
1 pound boneless venison loin
½ cup dry red wine
½ cup thinly sliced shallots
6 juniper berries or
 1½ tablespoons gin
1 teaspoon coarsely ground pepper

Cranberry Compote
1½ cups fresh cranberries
⅓ cup orange juice
¼ cup sugar
2 tablespoons thinly sliced shallots
1 tablespoon grated orange peel
1 teaspoon finely chopped peeled
 fresh ginger

1 cup canned unsalted beef broth

For venison: Place venison in medium bowl. Add wine, shallots, juniper berries and pepper; turn to coat meat. Cover and refrigerate overnight, turning twice.

For compote: Combine cranberries, orange juice, sugar, shallots, orange peel and ginger in heavy medium saucepan. Cook over medium-low heat until berries begin to pop and mixture boils, stirring occasionally, about 8 minutes. Transfer to bowl. Season with pepper. (*Can be prepared 1 day ahead. Cover and refrigerate. Bring to room temperature or gently reheat before serving.*)

Preheat oven to 400°F. Remove venison from marinade; pat dry. Reserve marinade. Heat heavy medium nonstick skillet over medium heat until drop of water evaporates on contact. Add venison and cook until well browned on all sides, about 6 minutes. Transfer to roasting pan. Roast to desired doneness, about 13 minutes for medium-rare. Transfer to carving board; tent with foil.

Add reserved marinade to roasting pan. Cook over medium-low heat until reduced to ½ cup, scraping up any browned bits, about 5 minutes. Add beef broth, increase heat to high and boil until reduced to ¾ cup, about 8 minutes. Strain sauce. Season with salt.

Cut venison across grain into thin slices. Arrange meat on platter. Add any accumulated juices from carving board to sauce. Drizzle some sauce over meat. Spoon compote alongside and serve, passing remaining sauce separately.

Chicken-stuffed Bell Peppers Spanish Style

Using leftover cooked chicken would save time here.

8 servings

2 cups diced cooked chicken
1 medium onion, chopped
1 cup packed grated sharp cheddar cheese (about 4 ounces)
¾ cup tomato sauce
1 4-ounce can chopped mild green chilies

2 large garlic cloves, minced
1½ teaspoons paprika
½ teaspoon cayenne pepper

8 yellow or green bell peppers

Combine first 8 ingredients in medium bowl. Season to taste with salt and pepper. (*Can be prepared 6 hours ahead. Cover and refrigerate.*)

Preheat oven to 375°F. Cut around stem of each bell pepper and remove, creating large opening at top. Scoop out seeds. Divide filling among peppers (about ½ cup each). Replace tops of peppers. Stand peppers in shallow casserole. Bake until filling is cooked through and peppers are tender, about 50 minutes.

Garlic-Lime Chicken

This tangy grilled chicken is good with black beans and tortillas.

6 servings

¾ cup fresh lime juice
½ cup chopped fresh cilantro
⅓ cup olive oil

4 garlic cloves, minced
6 chicken breast halves

Additional fresh cilantro

Combine first 4 ingredients in 9 × 13-inch baking dish. Add chicken and turn to coat. Rub lime mixture under chicken skin. Cover and refrigerate chicken 1 hour, turning occasionally.

Prepare barbecue (medium-high heat). Season chicken generously with salt and pepper. Grill until chicken is cooked through, turning occasionally, about 12 minutes. Transfer to platter; garnish with additional cilantro.

Chicken Tajine

There are hundreds of variations on the tajine, *a Moroccan stew that's traditionally cooked in a shallow clay pot with a tall lid. This is a take on one classic version that features chicken, lemon and olives.*

6 servings

3 tablespoons olive oil
2 3-pound chickens, quartered
2 onions, chopped
1 tablespoon plus 1 teaspoon paprika
2 teaspoons ground ginger
½ teaspoon turmeric
¼ teaspoon cayenne pepper
2 cups chicken stock or canned low-salt broth

3 lemons, each cut lengthwise into 6 pieces
1 cup Kalamata or other brine-cured olives (about 5 ounces)
1 cup pitted green olives (preferably imported)

Vegetable Couscous (see recipe)
Fresh cilantro

Heat olive oil in heavy large Dutch oven over high heat. Sprinkle chicken pieces with salt and pepper. Add to pan in batches and brown on both sides, about 5 minutes per side. Transfer to platter. Pour off all but thin film of fat. Add chopped onions and sauté over medium heat until tender, about 8 minutes. Add all spices and stir until fragrant, about 30 seconds. Return chicken pieces to pan. Add chicken stock and lemon pieces. Cover and simmer until chicken is cooked through, basting and turning occasionally, about 30 minutes. Add all olives. Season tajine to taste with salt and pepper. (*Can be prepared 1 day ahead. Cover and refrigerate. Reheat gently before continuing.*)

Mound couscous on platter. Surround with chicken and lemons. Spoon olives and some sauce over to moisten. Garnish with cilantro. Serve chicken, passing extra sauce separately.

Vegetable Couscous

6 servings

2 tablespoons olive oil
1 large onion, cut into chunks
1 large red bell pepper, cut into chunks
4 carrots, peeled, cut into ½-inch-thick rounds
2 zucchini, quartered lengthwise, cut into 1-inch pieces

2¼ cups chicken stock or canned broth
1 cup golden raisins
¾ teaspoon ground cinnamon
¼ teaspoon turmeric
1½ cups couscous (about 9 ounces)

Heat olive oil in heavy large saucepan over medium heat. Add onion and sauté 5 minutes. Add bell pepper and carrots and cook 5 minutes. Add zucchini and cook 5 minutes, stirring occasionally. Add chicken stock, golden raisins, ground cinnamon and turmeric. Season to taste with salt and pepper. Bring to boil. Mix in couscous. Cover, remove from heat and let stand 10 minutes. Fluff couscous with fork and serve immediately.

Moroccan-Style Cornish Game Hens

The hens should marinate at least 12 hours, so begin preparing this delicious main course a day before.

2 servings

1 large orange, thinly sliced
2 Cornish game hens, cut lengthwise in half
6 tablespoons chopped fresh cilantro
8 garlic cloves, finely chopped
1½ teaspoons ground cumin

½ cup tawny Port
¼ cup olive oil
¼ cup balsamic vinegar or red wine vinegar
2 tablespoons honey
20 whole pitted dates
10 large pitted green olives

Arrange orange slices in bottom of 9 × 13-inch glass baking dish. Top with game hens. Mix 4 tablespoons fresh cilantro, chopped garlic and 1¼ teaspoons cumin in bowl. Rub mixture all over hens. Whisk tawny Port, oil, vinegar and honey in small bowl. Pour over hens. Tuck dates and olives between hens. Season with salt and pepper. Cover and refrigerate 12 hours or overnight, turning once.

Preheat oven to 375°F. Turn hens skin side up. Bake hens with marinade, dates and olives until hens are cooked through, basting occasionally, about 40 minutes. Transfer hens, dates and olives to platter; discard orange slices. Pour pan juices into heavy small saucepan. Add remaining ¼ teaspoon cumin and boil until reduced to ½ cup, whisking frequently, about 5 minutes. Season with salt and pepper. Spoon some sauce over hens. Sprinkle with remaining 2 tablespoons chopped cilantro. Serve, passing remaining sauce separately.

Chinese Smoked Chicken

4 servings

6 tablespoons soy sauce
3 tablespoons hoisin sauce*
2 tablespoons dry white wine
1 green onion, chopped
1 tablespoon brown sugar
1 tablespoon finely minced ginger

1 teaspoon liquid smoke flavoring
1 cooking bag
1 3¾-pound chicken

Green onions, sliced
Steamed rice

Combine first 7 ingredients in cooking bag. Add chicken and seal tightly. Rotate bag to coat chicken with marinade. Refrigerate at least 3 hours or overnight, turning bag occasionally.

Preheat oven to 350°F. Set bag with chicken on baking sheet. Cut 5 small vents in top of bag. Bake until chicken is tender and brown, about 1 hour 15 minutes. Remove from oven and cool slightly. Open bag and pour juices into bowl. Cut chicken into pieces. Arrange on platter. Pour some of juices over chicken. Garnish with sliced green onions. Serve chicken with rice, passing remaining juices separately.

*Available at oriental markets and in the oriental section of some supermarkets.

Chicken with Goat Cheese and Roasted Bell Peppers

4 servings

½ red bell pepper
½ yellow bell pepper
3 ounces soft fresh goat cheese
  (such as Montrachet), cut into
  8 rounds
  Toasted sliced almonds

4 boneless skinless chicken breast
  halves
¼ cup plus 2 tablespoons olive oil

1 teaspoon chopped shallot
1 teaspoon chopped garlic
½ cup dry white wine
2 teaspoons chopped fresh
  rosemary or ½ teaspoon dried,
  crumbled
½ cup (1 stick) unsalted butter, cut
  into pieces

Preheat broiler. Arrange peppers cut side down on baking sheet. Broil until skin blackens. Transfer to bowl. Cover with foil and let stand 10 minutes to steam. Peel peppers and cut into strips. Coat cheese rounds with nuts. (*Can be prepared 1 day ahead. Cover peppers and cheese separately and refrigerate.*)

Prepare barbecue grill (medium-high heat) and preheat oven to 350°F. Brush chicken breast halves with 2 tablespoons olive oil. Grill just until cooked through, turning occasionally, about 10 minutes. Transfer chicken to baking sheet. Top with pepper strips and cheese rounds. Bake chicken just until cheese is heated through, about 5 minutes. Transfer to plates.

Meanwhile, heat remaining ¼ cup oil in heavy large skillet over high heat. Add shallot and garlic and sauté 30 seconds. Add wine and rosemary and boil until reduced by half, about 3 minutes. Gradually whisk in butter. Season sauce to taste with salt and pepper.

Spoon sauce over chicken and serve immediately.

Wine-braised Pork Loin

David Bishop

Swiss Cheese and Porcini Fondue and
Green Bean, Potato and Leek Salad

David Bishop

Beef Paprikas and Chocolate, Plum and Walnut Torte

David Bishop

*Roast Pesto Chicken; Parmesan Potatoes; Double Ginger
Gingerbread with Orange-Ginger Sauce*

Spencer Steaks with Red Wine-Shiitake Sauce; Fresh Corn and Cheddar Cheese Soufflé; Sundaes with Chocolate, Caramel and Macadamia Nut Sauce

Triple-Layer Devil's Food Cake

Ellen Silverman

Jennifer Cheung

Grilled Eggplant and Tomato Sandwiches

*Pears Poached in Spiced Red Wine
with Bow-Tie Pastries*

Kathlene Persoff

Roast Pesto Chicken

Pesto—a basil, pine nut and Parmesan sauce—is considered a staple by many cooks. Here it goes onto the bird and into the gravy of this dressed-up American standard.

4 servings

1 6½- to 7-pound roasting chicken
1 7-ounce container purchased pesto sauce
3 tablespoons dry white wine

¾ cup (about) plus 2 tablespoons canned low-salt chicken broth
2 tablespoons all purpose flour
3 tablespoons whipping cream
Fresh basil sprigs

Pat chicken dry. Slide hand between chicken skin and meat over breast and legs to form pockets. Reserve 1 tablespoon pesto for gravy; spread remaining pesto under skin and over breast and leg meat of chicken, in cavity of chicken and over outer skin. Tie legs together to hold shape. Tuck wings under body. Place chicken in large roasting pan. (*Can be made 4 hours ahead. Cover and chill.*)

Preheat oven to 450°F. Roast chicken 15 minutes. Reduce oven temperature to 375°F and roast until juices run clear when chicken is pierced in thickest part of thigh, basting occasionally with pan juices, about 1 hour 15 minutes. Transfer chicken to platter. Cover and keep warm.

Pour pan juices into glass measuring cup; degrease. Add wine to roasting pan and bring to boil, scraping up any browned bits. Add wine mixture and any drippings from platter to pan juices. Add enough broth to measure 1 cup. Transfer to heavy small saucepan. Combine 2 tablespoons broth and flour in bowl; stir until smooth. Add to saucepan. Bring to boil, whisking constantly. Boil until reduced to sauce consistency, stirring often, about 5 minutes. Mix in cream and reserved 1 tablespoon pesto. Season with salt and pepper. Garnish chicken with basil. Serve with gravy.

🍎 Fish and Shellfish

Swordfish with New-Wave Tartar Sauce

A low-fat tartar sauce makes this a fish dish for the nineties.

4 servings

⅔ cup reduced-calorie mayonnaise
⅓ cup plain low-fat yogurt
¼ cup chopped cornichons
2 tablespoons chopped fresh dill
2 teaspoons prepared horseradish
2 teaspoons Dijon mustard
1 tablespoon drained capers

4 6- to 8-ounce swordfish steaks (¾ inch thick)
Melted butter
Fresh lemon juice
Minced fresh dill
Fresh dill sprigs
Lemon wedges

Combine first 7 ingredients in medium bowl. Season to taste with salt and pepper. (*Tartar sauce can be prepared 2 days ahead. Cover and refrigerate.*)

Preheat broiler. Brush fish with butter; sprinkle with lemon juice. Season with salt and pepper. Broil until just cooked through, about 3 minutes per side. Transfer to plates. Sprinkle with minced dill. Garnish with dill sprigs and lemon wedges and serve with sauce.

Salmon with Arugula, Tomato and Caper Sauce

4 servings

1 pound plum tomatoes, seeded, chopped
¾ cup lightly packed chopped fresh arugula, basil or Italian parsley
½ cup olive oil
1 shallot, chopped

1½ tablespoons fresh lemon juice
1 tablespoon drained capers

4 6-ounce salmon fillets
Olive oil
Lemon wedges

Combine first 6 ingredients in medium bowl. Season with salt and pepper.

Preheat broiler. Brush both sides of salmon with oil; season with salt and pepper. Broil without turning until just cooked through, about 4 minutes. Transfer salmon to plates. Spoon tomato mixture over. Garnish with lemon wedges.

Whitefish with Spiced Pecans and Roasted Pepper Sauce

If whitefish is unavailable, use orange roughy instead in this delicious dish.

6 servings

Spiced Pecans
2 tablespoons Worcestershire sauce
1 tablespoon butter
2 teaspoons chili oil*
1 cup pecan halves (about 4 ounces)
¼ teaspoon dried thyme, crumbled
¼ teaspoon dried oregano, crumbled
¼ teaspoon salt
Pinch of cayenne pepper

Sauce
1 large red bell pepper

¼ cup white wine vinegar
¼ cup fresh lemon juice
2 tablespoons minced shallots

All purpose flour
6 8-ounce whitefish fillets
2 tablespoons olive oil

1 cup (2 sticks) butter, cut into pieces
Chopped fresh chives

For spiced pecans: Preheat oven to 350°F. Whisk Worcestershire sauce, butter and chili oil in heavy small ovenproof skillet over medium heat until butter melts. Add pecans, thyme, oregano, salt and cayenne and sauté 1 minute. Transfer skillet to oven and bake until pecans are dark brown, about 7 minutes. Transfer pecans to bowl.

For sauce: Char red bell pepper over gas flame or in broiler until blackened on all sides. Wrap bell pepper in paper bag and let stand 10 minutes. Peel and seed bell pepper. Rinse if necessary. Puree bell pepper in blender until smooth.

Boil white wine vinegar, fresh lemon juice and minced shallots in heavy small saucepan until reduced to 2 tablespoons liquid, about 4 minutes. Stir in ¼ cup pepper puree. (Reserve remaining puree for another use.) Remove from heat. (*Can be prepared 1 day ahead. Cover nuts and sauce separately. Chill sauce.*)

Place flour in large bowl. Season fish with salt and pepper. Dredge in flour, shaking off excess. Heat 1 tablespoon olive oil in heavy large skillet. Add 3 fish fillets and cook until opaque, about 3 minutes per side. Transfer to plates and keep warm. Repeat with remaining olive oil and fish fillets.

Meanwhile, warm sauce over low heat. Gradually whisk in butter. Season to taste with salt and pepper. Pour sauce around fish. Sprinkle fish with spiced pecans and chopped chives and serve.

*Available at Asian markets and in the Asian section of some supermarkets.

Sea Bass with Lentils and Olive Oil

4 servings

1⅓ cups lentils

3 tablespoons butter
1 onion, chopped
1 leek (white part only), sliced
1 celery stalk, sliced
1 garlic clove, pressed
5 cups chicken stock or canned broth

1 bouquet garni (1 bay leaf, 1 thyme sprig and 3 parsley stems, tied up in cheesecloth)

4 8-ounce sea bass fillets with skin (1½ to 2 inches thick)
¼ cup peanut oil

¼ cup olive oil
¼ cup dry white wine

Place lentils in large saucepan. Add enough cold water to cover by 3 inches. Let stand 6 hours. Drain lentils.

Melt 2 tablespoons butter in heavy large saucepan over medium heat. Add onion, leek, celery and garlic and sauté 10 minutes. Add chicken stock and bouquet garni and bring to boil. Add lentils, reduce heat and simmer mixture until tender, stirring occasionally, about 50 minutes. Remove bouquet garni. Stir in remaining 1 tablespoon butter. Set lentils aside.

Season sea bass fillets to taste with salt and pepper. Heat peanut oil in heavy large skillet over medium-high heat. Place fillets skin side down in skillet. Cook until opaque, turning once, about 6 minutes per side.

Meanwhile, combine olive oil and wine in heavy small saucepan. Cook over low heat just until heated through.

Spoon lentils onto plates. Top with fillets. Pour olive oil mixture over.

Poached Salmon with Lemon Mayonnaise

4 servings

Salmon
3 8-ounce bottles clam juice
¾ cup dry white wine
3 lemon slices
3 fresh dill sprigs
4 whole peppercorns
4 6- to 8-ounce salmon fillets

Mayonnaise
1 cup mayonnaise
2 tablespoons fresh lemon juice

2 teaspoons grated lemon peel
2 tablespoons chopped fresh chives
2 tablespoons chopped fresh parsley

Butter lettuce leaves
4 lemon slices
8 lemon wedges
Tomato wedges

For salmon: Combine first 5 ingredients in deep skillet. Simmer 10 minutes to blend flavors. Add salmon, cover and simmer until just cooked through, about 9 minutes per inch of thickness. Transfer salmon to plate, using 2 spatulas as aid. Reserve liquid in skillet. Cool salmon. Cover and chill until cold. (*Can be prepared up to 1 day ahead.*)

For mayonnaise: Boil salmon poaching liquid in skillet until reduced to ¼ cup, about 20 minutes. Combine mayonnaise, lemon juice, lemon peel, chives and parsley in medium bowl. Mix in 1 tablespoon poaching liquid. Season to taste with pepper. (*Can be prepared 1 day ahead. Cover and chill.*)

Line platter with lettuce. Top with salmon. Make cut in each lemon slice from center to edge. Twist lemon slices and place atop salmon. Garnish with lemon wedges and tomatoes and serve with mayonnaise.

Gingered Shrimp with Asian Noodles

2 servings

3 ounces bean thread vermicelli (cellophane noodles)*
4 teaspoons oriental sesame oil

2 tablespoons rice vinegar
2 tablespoons chopped fresh cilantro
2 tablespoons minced seasoned sliced ginger (also known as sushi ginger)*

1 tablespoon minced pickled jalapeño chilies
2 teaspoons honey
12 ounces uncooked medium shrimp, peeled, deveined, tails left intact
4 green onions, sliced
2 garlic cloves, minced
2 teaspoons cornstarch
½ cup water

Cook noodles in large pot of boiling water until just tender but still firm to bite, stirring occasionally. Drain. Transfer to bowl. Add 2 teaspoons sesame oil to noodles and toss to coat.

Mix vinegar, cilantro, ginger, jalapeños and honey in small bowl. Season shrimp with salt and pepper. Heat remaining 2 teaspoons sesame oil in heavy large skillet over medium-high heat. Add green onions and garlic; sauté until aromatic, about 3 minutes. Add vinegar mixture and shrimp to skillet; stir until shrimp are just cooked through, about 3 minutes. Dissolve cornstarch in ½ cup water. Add mixture to skillet; stir until liquid thickens, about 2 minutes.

Mound noodles on platter. Arrange shrimp over and serve.

*Available at Asian markets and in the Asian section of many supermarkets.

Swordfish Tacos

4 servings

1 pound ¾-inch-thick swordfish steaks
Olive oil
Warm corn tortillas

Lime wedges
Thinly sliced cabbage
Pico de Gallo (see recipe)
Sour cream

Prepare barbecue (medium-high heat) or preheat broiler. Brush swordfish generously with olive oil and season with salt and pepper. Grill or broil until just cooked through, about 4 minutes per side. Transfer steaks to plate and cut into chunks. Serve swordfish with corn tortillas, lime wedges, cabbage, Pico de Gallo and sour cream, allowing guests to assemble their own tacos.

Pico de Gallo

Besides the tacos, try this salsa on scrambled eggs, grilled chicken or on a baked potato.

Makes about 3 cups

2 large tomatoes, diced
1 bunch green onions, thinly sliced
2 jalapeño chilies, seeded, diced

2 tablespoons olive oil
1 tablespoon red wine vinegar

Combine all ingredients in bowl. Season to taste with salt. (*Can be prepared 6 hours ahead. Store at room temperature.*)

Salmon with Breadcrumb Crust and Dill Sauce

6 servings

Sauce
1½ cups dry vermouth
¼ cup chopped leek (white part only)
3 shallots or green onions, chopped
2½ cups whipping cream

Fish
2 cups fresh white breadcrumbs
2 tablespoons chopped fresh dill or 2 teaspoons dried dillweed
1 teaspoon prepared horseradish

¼ cup (½ stick) unsalted butter, melted, cooled
3 tablespoons olive oil
6 6-ounce 1-inch-thick salmon fillets

2 bunches fresh spinach, stemmed

¼ cup chopped fresh dill or 1 tablespoon dried dillweed
1 teaspoon fresh lemon juice

For sauce: Combine first 3 ingredients in heavy medium saucepan. Boil until liquid is reduced to 3 tablespoons, stirring occasionally, about 20 minutes. Add cream and boil until sauce is reduced to 1½ cups, about 15 minutes. Strain sauce. Season with salt and pepper. (*Can be made 1 day ahead. Cover and chill.*)

For fish: Preheat oven to 350°F. Mix first 3 ingredients in medium bowl. Add butter and mix with fingertips to form coarse crumbs. Heat 2 tablespoons oil in heavy large skillet over medium-high heat. Add fish and cook until golden brown, about 3 minutes per side. Using metal spatula, transfer fish to baking sheet; cool. Sprinkle breadcrumb mixture over fish; press gently with fingertips to adhere. Bake fish until firm to touch, about 10 minutes.

Meanwhile, heat remaining 1 tablespoon oil in heavy large skillet over high heat. Add spinach and cook until wilted, stirring frequently.

Preheat broiler. Transfer fish to broiler; broil until crust browns, about 1 minute. Divide spinach among plates. Top with fish. Bring sauce to simmer. Mix in dill and lemon juice. Season with salt and pepper. Ladle sauce around fish. Serve immediately.

Sautéed Shrimp with Gorgonzola Sauce

2 servings

16 large uncooked shrimp, peeled, deveined, tails intact
   All purpose flour (for dredging)
1 tablespoon butter
2 tablespoons brandy
⅓ cup whipping cream

⅓ cup packed crumbled Gorgonzola cheese (about 1½ ounces)
⅓ cup grated Parmesan cheese (about 1 ounce)
1½ teaspoons minced fresh marjoram or ½ teaspoon dried, crumbled

Coat shrimp with flour; shake off excess. Melt butter in heavy large skillet over high heat. Add shrimp and sauté 1 minute. Add brandy and cook 30 seconds. Add cream, Gorgonzola, Parmesan and marjoram and boil until shrimp are cooked through and sauce thickens, stirring frequently and turning shrimp with tongs, 3 minutes. Divide shrimp between plates. Spoon sauce over.

Grilled Salmon with Avocado-Citrus Salsa

12 servings

2 oranges
2 small onions, diced
2 cups chopped fresh pineapple
2 large tomatoes, peeled, seeded, chopped
½ cup vegetable oil
½ cup chopped fresh cilantro
6 small serrano chilies,* minced

12 6-ounce 1½-inch-thick center-cut salmon fillets with skin
3 cups pink grapefruit juice

1 avocado, halved, pitted, diced
   Fresh cilantro sprigs

Cut off peel and white pith from oranges. Using small sharp knife, cut between membranes to release orange segments. Cut each segment in half and place in bowl. Add onions, pineapple, tomatoes, oil, cilantro and chilies. (*Can be made 8 hours ahead. Cover and refrigerate.*)

Place salmon in shallow baking dish. Pour grapefruit juice over. Let stand 1 hour at room temperature, turning occasionally.

Prepare barbecue (medium-high heat). Place salmon skin side down on grill. Cover and cook until just opaque, about 7 minutes. Transfer salmon to platter. Mix avocado into salsa and spoon over salmon. Garnish with cilantro.

*A very hot, small fresh green chili available at Latin American markets and many supermarkets.

🍎 Eggs, Cheese and Vegetables

Mushroom and Cheese Frittata

2 servings

2 tablespoons (¼ stick) butter
6 ounces mushrooms, sliced
4 large eggs

2 green onions, sliced
2 8 × 4-inch slices Swiss cheese
(about 2 ounces)

Preheat broiler. Melt butter in heavy 10-inch nonstick skillet over medium heat. Add mushrooms and sauté until golden brown, about 8 minutes. Beat eggs and green onions to blend in bowl. Season with salt and pepper. Pour egg mixture over mushrooms and stir briefly. Let eggs begin to set around edges. Lift edges and tilt pan, letting uncooked portion flow under cooked eggs. Cook until eggs are almost set but still slightly moist, about 30 seconds. Arrange cheese slices atop frittata. Broil until cheese melts and bubbles. Slide frittata onto plate.

Vegetable Paella

A low-fat rendition of the classic dish.

6 servings

½ cup water
¼ teaspoon saffron threads

2 tablespoons olive oil
1 red bell pepper, diced
1 medium onion, diced
½ 9-ounce package frozen baby artichokes, thawed, quartered
2 large garlic cloves, minced
1½ cups paella rice,* Arborio rice* or medium-grain white rice
3 cups chicken stock or canned low-salt broth

2 cups chopped escarole or chard
1 cup drained canned ready-cut tomatoes
¾ teaspoon paprika
½ teaspoon salt
1 15-ounce can cannellini (white kidney beans), rinsed, drained
½ cup shelled fresh peas or frozen peas

Bring water to boil in small saucepan. Add saffron, cover and remove from heat. Let stand 10 minutes.

Heat olive oil in heavy large saucepan over medium-high heat. Add bell pepper and onion and sauté until onion is golden, about 8 minutes. Add artichokes and garlic and sauté 5 minutes. Reduce heat to low. Add rice and stir to coat with oil. Add chicken stock, escarole and tomatoes and bring to boil, stirring frequently. Add saffron water, paprika and salt. Reduce heat to medium-low. Cover and cook 15 minutes. Mix beans and peas into rice, cover and continue cooking mixture until liquid is absorbed and rice is tender, about 5 minutes. Remove saucepan from heat. Let stand 5 minutes and serve.

*Paella rice and Arborio rice are short-grain varieties. They are available at specialty foods stores and also at some supermarkets.

Huevos Oaxaca

4 servings

Corn oil (for deep frying)
6 corn tortillas, halved

12 eggs
4 large green onions, sliced
2 jalapeño chilies, very thinly sliced
½ red bell pepper, diced

¼ cup chopped fresh cilantro
1½ teaspoons ground cumin
4 ounces feta cheese, crumbled

2 tablespoons corn oil
Fresh cilantro sprigs

Heat oil in heavy large saucepan to 375°F. Add tortilla halves and fry until golden brown and crisp, turning occasionally, about 2 minutes. Transfer to paper towels and drain.

Beat eggs, next 5 ingredients and half of cheese in bowl. Crumble in 4 tortilla halves. Season to taste with salt and pepper. Let stand 5 minutes.

Heat 2 tablespoons oil in heavy large skillet over medium heat. Add egg mixture and cook until just set, stirring frequently, about 3 minutes. Divide among plates. Sprinkle remaining cheese over eggs. Stand 2 tortilla halves in each serving and garnish with cilantro sprigs.

Orange French Toast

4 servings

5 large eggs
3 tablespoons whipping cream
3 tablespoons pure maple syrup
3 tablespoons orange juice
3 tablespoons triple sec or other orange liqueur

¼ teaspoon ground cinnamon
⅛ teaspoon ground nutmeg
4 1½-inch-thick egg bread slices

2 tablespoons (about) unsalted butter
Pure maple syrup

Whisk first 7 ingredients in large shallow dish. Add bread slices and turn to coat. Cover and refrigerate until bread absorbs egg mixture, turning occasionally, approximately 1 hour.

Preheat oven to warm. Melt 1 tablespoon butter in heavy large skillet over medium heat. Add 2 egg bread slices. Cover and cook until deep golden brown, about 5 minutes per side. Transfer to cookie sheet. Keep warm in oven. Repeat with remaining bread slices, adding more butter to skillet as necessary. Transfer French toast to plates. Serve with maple syrup.

Potato Omelet with Olives

2 servings

1 8-ounce russet potato

2 tablespoons olive oil
½ small onion, chopped
¼ small green bell pepper, diced
¼ cup sliced pimiento-stuffed green Spanish olives

1 tablespoon minced fresh oregano or 1 teaspoon dried, crumbled
¾ cup shredded manchego or white cheddar cheese (about 2½ ounces)

6 eggs

Boil russet potato in salted water until just tender when pierced with sharp knife, about 25 minutes. Drain potato. Cool, peel and dice.

Heat 1 tablespoon olive oil in heavy medium saucepan over medium-high heat. Add onion and bell pepper and sauté until onion is golden brown and pepper is tender, about 10 minutes. Mix in potato, Spanish olives and oregano and cook until mixture is heated through, stirring occasionally, about 5 minutes. Remove from heat. Gently mix in cheese. Season to taste with salt and pepper and cover to keep warm.

Heat remaining 1 tablespoon olive oil in heavy 10-inch nonstick skillet over medium-high heat. Beat eggs to blend in large bowl. Season with salt and pepper. Add eggs to skillet. Stir with back of fork and lift edges, allowing uncooked portion of eggs to flow under cooked portion. Cook until eggs are just set, about 3 minutes. Spoon filling over half of eggs. Using spatula, fold unfilled portion of eggs over filling. Transfer to platter.

Three-Alarm Tofu and Mushroom Stir-Fry

Tofu makes the perfect foil for the Asian flavors in this colorful and spicy dish.

4 servings

8 ounces tofu (preferably regular), drained, cut into ½-inch cubes
¼ cup canned low-salt chicken broth
1 teaspoon cornstarch
1 tablespoon low-sodium soy sauce
1 tablespoon honey
1 teaspoon oriental sesame oil
½ teaspoon dried crushed red pepper

4 tablespoons vegetable oil
10 ounces button mushrooms, quartered
7 ounces fresh shiitake mushrooms, stemmed, chopped
1 tablespoon minced peeled fresh ginger
1 tablespoon minced garlic
1 tablespoon minced jalapeño chili with seeds
½ cup diced red bell pepper
½ cup thinly sliced green onion tops
Freshly cooked rice

Place tofu cubes on double-thick layer of paper towels. Let drain 20 minutes. Whisk broth and cornstarch in medium bowl until cornstarch dissolves. Mix in soy sauce, honey, sesame oil and crushed red pepper. Set mixture aside.

Heat 2 tablespoons vegetable oil in wok or heavy large skillet over high heat. Add tofu and stir-fry until golden brown, about 4 minutes. Transfer tofu to plate using slotted spoon. Add remaining 2 tablespoons oil to wok and set over high heat. Add all mushrooms and stir-fry until golden, about 5 minutes. Add ginger, garlic and chili and stir-fry 1 minute. Add tofu, bell pepper and green onion and stir-fry 1 minute. Season with salt and pepper. Stir broth mixture, add to wok and bring to boil, stirring constantly. Spoon rice onto plates and top with vegetable stir-fry. Serve immediately.

Swiss Cheese and Porcini Fondue

6 servings

1 ounce dried porcini mushrooms*
1½ cups hot water

½ pound Emmenthal cheese, grated
½ pound Swiss Gruyère cheese, grated
1 tablespoon cornstarch

1 cup dry white wine
1 garlic clove, halved
2 teaspoons minced fresh thyme
   Fresh thyme leaves
   Day-old French bread, cut into 1-inch cubes

Soak porcini mushrooms in 1½ cups hot water until softened, about 20 minutes. Drain, reserving soaking liquid. Squeeze mushrooms dry. Chop.

Mix Emmenthal and Gruyère cheeses and cornstarch in large bowl. Combine 1 cup reserved mushroom soaking liquid, white wine and garlic in fondue pot or heavy medium saucepan. Simmer 2 minutes. Discard garlic. Adjust heat so that liquid barely simmers. Add cheese 1 handful at a time and stir until each addition melts before adding next. After all cheese is added, mix until smooth. Mix in mushrooms and 2 teaspoons minced fresh thyme. Season with generous amount of pepper. (*Can be prepared 1 day ahead. Cool. Press plastic onto surface of fondue and refrigerate. Cover and refrigerate remaining mushroom soaking liquid. Before continuing, rewarm fondue over low heat, stirring frequently and adding reserved mushroom soaking liquid as necessary if fondue is too thick.*) If not using fondue pot, transfer mixture to flameproof 2-quart casserole. Sprinkle with fresh thyme leaves. Set over alcohol burner or gas table burner and serve, allowing diners to skewer bread with fork and dip into cheese fondue.

*Porcini mushrooms are available at Italian markets and specialty foods stores.

5 ❧ *Vegetables, Grains and Breads*

Nutrition made the news in 1992, last spring in particular when the U.S. Department of Agriculture introduced its new Food Guide Pyramid. The idea behind the Pyramid is to help us all learn more about what foods we need, from what groups and in what amounts. It is interesting to note that the Pyramid recommends we eat three to five servings a day of vegetables, and a whopping six to eleven servings from the rice, bread, cereal and pasta group. To help you get started on the road to good health, here are more than twenty vegetable, grain and bread recipes.

If one vegetable is good for you, then three could only be better, as in the Vegetable Stir-Fry, a crunchy, colorful and healthful sauté featuring red cabbage, green beans and carrots. For potato fans, there are a number of delicious new recipes here, including Mashed Potatoes with Cabbage and Cheddar Cheese, Whipped Potatoes with Olive Oil and Parmesan and Coriander Potatoes.

Grains turn up for breakfast in the do-ahead Mixed Grain and Wild Rice Cereal, which you can keep in the refrigerator and reheat, a single serving at a time, in the microwave. For a new approach to rice, try Corn Risotto, made with the Italian short-grained rice called Arborio—great as a side dish for roasted chicken or meat.

Bread lovers will find plenty to choose from here, including a couple of delicious corn breads, some wonderfully rich scones and good-for-you Raspberry Bran Muffins.

❧ Vegetables

Gratin of Turnips, Yams and Potatoes

4 servings

2 tablespoons butter
1 large onion, chopped
1 pound russet potatoes, peeled, thinly sliced
1 12-ounce yam, peeled, thinly sliced

1 8-ounce turnip, peeled, thinly sliced
1 cup chicken stock or canned low-salt broth
1 cup dry vermouth

Preheat oven to 375°F. Melt butter in heavy large saucepan over medium heat. Add onion and sauté until tender, about 8 minutes. Add potatoes, yam, turnip, stock and vermouth. Season generously with salt and pepper. Bring to boil. Cover, reduce heat to low and simmer vegetables 15 minutes.

Butter 8 × 8-inch baking dish with 2-inch-high sides. Transfer vegetables and liquid to dish. Bake until vegetables are tender and most liquid is absorbed, about 1 hour. Let stand 10 minutes.

Vegetable Stir-Fry

A crunchy, colorful and healthful sauté featuring red cabbage, green beans and carrots.

8 servings

1 pound green beans, trimmed
4 large carrots, peeled, sliced medium-thin on diagonal
½ small head red cabbage, halved, then cut crosswise into ½-inch-wide pieces
3 tablespoons vegetable oil

4 fresh ginger slices
½ teaspoon salt
3 tablespoons canned chicken broth or water
2 tablespoons fresh lime juice
2 teaspoons oriental sesame oil

Cook beans and carrots in large pot of boiling salted water until just crisp-tender, about 4 minutes. Drain. (*Can be prepared 1 day ahead. Refrigerate. Bring to room temperature before continuing.*)

Rinse cabbage and drain well just before cooking. Heat vegetable oil in wok or heavy large skillet over high heat. Add ginger; press and stir until aromatic. Add cabbage and stir to coat with oil. Sprinkle with ½ teaspoon salt. Add broth, reduce heat to low, cover and cook 2 minutes. Uncover, increase heat to high, add green beans and carrots and stir-fry until heated through. Mix in lime juice and sesame oil. Season to taste with salt and pepper. Discard ginger and serve.

Coriander Potatoes

6 servings

6 russet potatoes, cut into rounds
3 tablespoons olive oil

2¼ teaspoons ground coriander
Chopped fresh cilantro

Preheat oven to 350°F. Mix potatoes and oil in large bowl. Season generously with salt and pepper. Transfer to large baking sheet. Bake until tender and brown, turning after 30 minutes, about 45 minutes. Transfer to large bowl. Mix in coriander and cilantro and serve.

Fresh Corn and Cheddar Cheese Soufflé

4 servings

4 tablespoons (½ stick) butter
1 cup fresh corn kernels (from about 2 ears) or frozen, thawed
3 tablespoons all purpose flour
1 cup milk
4 egg yolks
½ teaspoon dry mustard

½ teaspoon salt
¾ cup grated sharp cheddar cheese
1 bunch fresh chives, chopped

5 egg whites

Preheat oven to 400°F. Butter 8-cup soufflé dish. Melt 1 tablespoon butter in heavy medium skillet over medium heat. Add corn and sauté until tender, about 3 minutes. Remove from heat. Melt 3 tablespoons butter in heavy medium saucepan over medium heat. Add flour and stir 3 minutes. Gradually whisk in milk. Boil until very thick, stirring constantly, about 1 minute. Remove from heat. Whisk in yolks 1 at a time. Whisk in mustard and salt. Season with pepper. (*Can be made 2 hours ahead. Dot top with butter and let stand at room temperature. Before continuing, rewarm over low heat until just lukewarm, stirring constantly.*) Add corn, cheese and chives.

Using clean dry beaters, beat whites and pinch of salt until stiff but not dry. Stir ¼ of whites into yolk mixture to lighten. Gently fold in remaining whites. Spoon into prepared dish. Place in oven. Reduce temperature to 375°F and bake until puffed and golden on top and soufflé still moves slightly when top is gently touched, about 30 minutes. Serve hot.

Whipped Potatoes with Olive Oil and Parmesan

6 servings

2 pounds russet potatoes
¾ cup (or more) hot canned chicken broth
6 tablespoons olive oil

¾ cup grated Parmesan cheese
½ cup chopped fresh chives
Additional grated Parmesan cheese

Bring large pot of water to boil. Add potatoes and cook until tender. Drain. Peel potatoes and transfer to large bowl. Add ¾ cup broth. Using electric mixer, beat potato mixture until smooth. Gradually beat in oil and then ¾ cup cheese, adding more broth if very thick. Stir in chives. Season with salt and pepper. Garnish with additional grated cheese.

Roasted Onions and Potatoes

8 servings

2 pounds russet potatoes, scrubbed, cut into wedges
2 onions, cut into chunks
⅓ cup olive oil
¼ cup (½ stick) butter, melted
1 envelope onion soup mix (half of 2.4-ounce package)

1 teaspoon dried thyme, crumbled
1 teaspoon dried oregano, crumbled
1 teaspoon dried marjoram, crumbled

Preheat oven to 450°F. Combine all ingredients in large roasting pan. Toss well. Bake until potatoes are crisp and golden brown, stirring occasionally, about 1 hour 10 minutes. Season potatoes to taste with salt and pepper.

Mashed Potatoes with Cabbage and Cheddar Cheese

8 servings

½ large head green cabbage, thinly
   sliced (about 8 cups)
2½ pounds russet potatoes, peeled,
   coarsely chopped
½ cup (1 stick) unsalted butter,
   cut into pieces

¼ cup chopped fresh chives or
   green onion tops
1 cup packed grated cheddar cheese
   (about 4 ounces)

Butter eight 1-cup soufflé dishes or one 8-cup baking dish. Cook cabbage in
large pot of boiling salted water until tender, about 2 minutes. Transfer to bowl
using slotted spoon; drain. Return water in pot to boil. Add potatoes and cook
until tender. Drain; return potatoes to pot. Add butter and mash with potato
masher. Mix in chives, then cabbage. Season to taste with salt and pepper.
Spoon potato mixture into prepared dishes. Sprinkle with cheese. (*Can be prepared 2 hours ahead. Cover and let stand at room temperature.*)
   Preheat oven to 350°F. Bake potatoes until heated through and cheese bubbles, about 25 minutes for soufflé dishes or 35 minutes for baking dish.

Fiesta Zucchini

4 servings

2 tablespoons olive oil
1 pound zucchini (about 3),
   quartered lengthwise, cut
   crosswise into ½-inch-wide pieces
3 garlic cloves, minced

¼ teaspoon dried oregano,
   crumbled
½ cup purchased salsa
½ cup shredded Monterey Jack
   cheese

Heat olive oil in heavy medium skillet over medium-low heat. Add zucchini,
garlic and oregano and sauté until garlic is just golden, about 2 minutes. Add
salsa and simmer until zucchini is just tender, about 6 minutes. Reduce heat to
low. Sprinkle Jack cheese over zucchini. Cover and cook until cheese melts,
approximately 2 minutes. Serve.

Parmesan Potatoes

4 servings

4 large russet potatoes, each cut
   lengthwise into eighths
¼ cup olive oil

1 teaspoon dried crushed red pepper
½ cup grated Parmesan cheese
   Chopped fresh basil

Position rack in lowest third of oven and preheat to 375°F. Place potatoes in
roasting pan. Add oil and red pepper and toss to coat. Season with salt and
pepper. Bake until tender on inside and crusty on outside, turning once, about
1 hour. Sprinkle with Parmesan and basil.

🍎 Grains

Wild Rice with Mushrooms

4 servings

½ cup (about 4 ounces) wild rice
2 cups canned low-salt chicken broth

6 tablespoons (¾ stick) butter
1 pound mushrooms, sliced

1 teaspoon dried rosemary, crumbled
¼ teaspoon rubbed dried sage
Pinch of cayenne pepper
¼ cup dry Sherry

Combine wild rice and chicken broth in heavy medium saucepan. Cover and simmer over low heat until rice is tender and liquid is absorbed, about 1 hour. Remove rice from heat.

Melt butter in heavy large skillet over medium-high heat. Add mushrooms, rosemary, sage and cayenne and sauté until mushrooms are golden brown, about 12 minutes. Add Sherry and stir until mushrooms are dry, scraping any browned bits from bottom of skillet, about 2 minutes. Add rice and stir until well mixed and rice is heated through, about 2 minutes. Season to taste with salt and pepper.

Stir-fried Rice with Vegetables

4 servings

2 tablespoons low-sodium soy sauce
1 tablespoon oyster sauce*
2 teaspoons oriental sesame oil
2 teaspoons minced garlic
2 teaspoons minced peeled fresh ginger
1 tablespoon dry sake or canned low-salt chicken broth
½ cup matchstick-size strips red bell pepper
½ cup matchstick-size strips carrot

½ cup matchstick-size strips leek (white and light green parts)
½ cup matchstick-size strips fresh shiitake mushrooms, stems removed (about 1 ounce)
2 cups cooked brown rice, room temperature
2 tablespoons water
1 tablespoon chopped fresh cilantro
1 teaspoon minced green onion

Combine soy sauce and oyster sauce in small bowl. Heat wok or heavy large skillet (preferably nonstick) over high heat until drop of water evaporates on contact. Add sesame oil; heat 10 seconds. Add garlic and ginger; stir-fry 10 seconds. Add sake or broth, bell pepper, carrot, leek and mushrooms and stir-fry until crisp-tender, about 2 minutes. Transfer to plate. Add rice to hot wok. Sprinkle with 2 tablespoons water; stir-fry until rice is heated through, about 2 minutes. Mix in soy and oyster sauce mixture. Return vegetables to wok and stir until hot. Transfer to serving dish. Garnish with cilantro and green onion.

*Oyster sauce is available at Asian markets and most supermarkets.

Mixed Grain and Wild Rice Cereal

Prepare a batch of this breakfast dish and store it in the refrigerator. Then simply reheat single servings in the microwave.

8 servings

8	cups water
½	cup wild rice
½	cup pearl barley
½	cup steel-cut oats (Irish oatmeal)
½	cup bulgur wheat
½	cup raisins

½	cup chopped pitted dates
¼	cup plus 2 tablespoons firmly packed dark brown sugar
3	tablespoons butter
¾	teaspoon salt
½	teaspoon ground cinnamon

Simmer 2 cups water and wild rice in small saucepan 20 minutes. Drain.

Preheat oven to 375°F. Butter 2½-quart ovenproof dish. In prepared dish, mix wild rice with remaining 6 cups water. Stir in all remaining ingredients. Cover loosely with foil and bake until grains are tender, water is absorbed and cereal is creamy, stirring occasionally, about 1½ hours.

Indonesian Spiced Rice

Turmeric adds color and chilies add heat to this superb side dish.

8 servings

3	tablespoons peanut oil
1	large onion, chopped
2	jalapeño chilies, seeded but not deveined, minced
1	teaspoon turmeric
½	teaspoon ground cinnamon

1	pound long-grain white rice
2	14½-ounce cans chicken broth
⅓	cup water
1	bay leaf
	Chopped green onion tops

Heat oil in heavy large saucepan over medium-low heat. Add chopped onion and chilies and stir until onion is translucent, about 8 minutes. Mix in turmeric and ground cinnamon. Add rice and stir 2 minutes. Add chicken broth, water and bay leaf. Bring to boil. Reduce heat to low, cover and cook until liquid is absorbed, about 20 minutes. Sprinkle with green onions and serve.

Rice with Lemongrass and Green Onion

4 servings

2	tablespoons vegetable oil
⅔	cup finely chopped onion
¼	teaspoon turmeric
1	cup long-grain white rice
1¾	cups water

2	12-inch-long lemongrass stalks, cut into 2-inch-long pieces
½	teaspoon salt
1	large green onion, chopped

Heat 1½ tablespoons oil in heavy medium saucepan over medium heat. Add ⅔ cup onion and turmeric and sauté 5 minutes. Mix in rice. Add water, lemongrass and ½ teaspoon salt and bring to simmer. Cover, reduce heat to medium-low and simmer until rice is tender and liquid is absorbed, about 18 minutes. Remove from heat; let stand covered 10 minutes. Discard lemongrass.

Heat remaining ½ tablespoon oil in heavy large skillet over medium heat. Add green onion and sauté 1 minute. Add rice and stir until heated through. Season to taste with salt. Serve immediately.

Corn Risotto

Great with roasted chicken or meat.

4 servings

3 cups fresh corn kernels (from about 4 ears) or frozen, thawed

¼ cup (½ stick) butter
3 tablespoons chopped shallots
½ cup Arborio rice* or medium-grain rice

¼ cup dry white wine
3 cups (or more) chicken stock or canned broth
⅓ cup grated Parmesan cheese

Puree 2 cups corn kernels in blender. Set corn puree aside.

Melt butter in heavy medium saucepan over medium heat. Add chopped shallots and sauté until translucent, about 5 minutes. Mix in rice and cook 1 minute, stirring constantly. Add dry white wine and cook until all liquid is absorbed, about 4 minutes. Add 3 cups chicken stock and cook 10 minutes, stirring occasionally. Increase heat and boil until rice is thick and creamy, stirring occasionally, about 10 minutes. Add corn puree, remaining 1 cup corn kernels and grated Parmesan cheese. Cook rice 3 minutes. Thin rice with more chicken stock if necessary. Season risotto to taste with salt and pepper and serve.

*Arborio, an Italian short-grain rice, is available at Italian markets and many specialty foods stores.

❦ *Breads*

Green Onion-Sesame Biscuits

Makes about 10

2 cups unbleached all purpose flour
3 large green onions, thinly sliced
1 tablespoon baking powder
2 medium garlic cloves, pressed
1 teaspooon salt

1 cup (or more) whipping cream
½ teaspoon oriental sesame oil
1 egg, beaten to blend (glaze)
Sesame seeds

Preheat oven to 375°F. Mix first 5 ingredients in large bowl. Combine 1 cup cream and sesame oil in small bowl. Mix into dry ingredients. Add enough additional cream by tablespoons to bind dough. Knead 30 seconds. Flatten dough into ½-inch-thick round. Cut out biscuits using 2½-inch-diameter cookie cutter dipped into flour. Gather scraps and reform into round. Cut out additional biscuits. Transfer to baking sheet. Brush with glaze. Top with sesame seeds. Bake until biscuits rise and tops are brown, about 35 minutes. Cool slightly.

❦

Blue Cheese Bread

12 servings

8 ounces blue cheese
1 cup (2 sticks) unsalted butter, room temperature

2 French bread baguettes or 4 sourdough flutes (2 pounds total), halved lengthwise
Chopped celery tops

Blend cheese and butter in processor until smooth. (*Can be prepared 2 days ahead. Cover and refrigerate. Bring to room temperature before using.*)

Preheat broiler. Broil bread crust side up until crisp. Turn and broil cut side until light brown. Spread cheese mixture over cut side of bread. Sprinkle liberally with pepper. Broil until cheese bubbles and begins to brown. Remove from broiler and sprinkle bread with celery. Cut crosswise into 1-inch pieces.

Rosemary-Olive Focaccia

Frozen bread dough makes this a snap to prepare.

4 servings

1 pound frozen bread dough, thawed
3 tablespoons olive oil
1 tablespoon minced fresh rosemary or 1 teaspoon dried, crumbled

¾ cup (about) grated Parmesan cheese
6 Kalamata olives,* pitted, quartered
4 oil-packed sun-dried tomatoes, drained, cut into strips
2 large garlic cloves, thinly sliced
Fresh rosemary sprigs (optional)

Preheat oven to 450°F. Place bread dough in bowl. Add 1 tablespoon oil and minced rosemary. Season generously with pepper. Knead dough until ingredients are thoroughly combined.

Roll dough out on lightly floured work surface to 9 × 6-inch rectangle. Transfer to baking sheet. Flatten and press dough into 12 × 9-inch rectangle. Rub 1 tablespoon olive oil over. Sprinkle ½ cup Parmesan cheese over; press gently into dough. Bake until bread is almost cooked through and cheese begins to brown, about 12 minutes. Arrange Kalamata olives, sun-dried tomatoes and garlic atop bread. Sprinkle enough remaining Parmesan cheese over to cover lightly. Drizzle remaining 1 tablespoon olive oil over. Top with rosemary sprigs. Continue baking until cheese melts and bread is cooked through, about 5 minutes more. Cut into squares or wedges and serve.

*Black, brine-cured olives, available at Greek and Italian markets and some supermarkets.

Peppered Corn Bread

Makes 1 loaf

1½ cups cornmeal
1½ teaspoons pepper
1½ teaspoons salt
1 cup boiling water
1 package rapid-rise yeast
1 teaspoon sugar

¼ cup hot water (125°F to 130°F)
1 tablespoon olive oil
2 cups (about) bread flour

Olive oil

Mix 1 cup cornmeal, pepper and salt in large bowl of electric mixer fitted with dough hook. Add 1 cup boiling water and mix until smooth. Let cool to 120°F, about 20 minutes. Mix in yeast and sugar, then ¼ cup hot water and 1 table-spoon oil. Mix in remaining ½ cup cornmeal. Add 1 cup flour and mix until smooth and elastic, about 5 minutes.

Cover bowl with damp towel and let dough rise in warm draft-free area until puffy, about 45 minutes.

Grease 9-inch metal pie pan with oil. Knead enough bread flour into dough to make it nonsticky. Knead on floured surface until smooth and elastic, about 5 minutes. Knead into ball. Place in pan. Flatten to fill bottom of pan. Cover with towel; let rise in warm draft-free area until doubled, about 50 minutes.

Preheat oven to 350°F. Score top of bread in ticktacktoe pattern. Bake until bread is light brown on top and sounds hollow when tapped on bottom, about 45 minutes. Remove from pan; cool on rack. Serve warm or at room tempera-ture. (*Can be made 1 day ahead. Cool. Wrap tightly. Before serving, wrap in foil and warm in 350°F oven 15 minutes.*)

Buttermilk Scones

8 servings

2 cups all purpose flour
⅓ cup sugar
1½ teaspoons baking powder
½ teaspoon baking soda
¼ teaspoon salt

6 tablespoons (¾ stick) chilled unsalted butter, cut into pieces
⅔ cup buttermilk
2 large eggs
1½ teaspoons vanilla extract

Preheat oven to 350°F. Grease large cookie sheet. Mix first 5 ingredients in large bowl. Add butter and rub with fingertips until mixture resembles fine meal. Whisk buttermilk, eggs and vanilla in medium bowl to blend. Gradually add to flour and stir until moist clumps form. Turn dough out onto lightly floured surface. Knead 4 times to blend. Transfer dough to prepared cookie sheet. Press dough into 8-inch round. Using small sharp knife, score dough into 8 wedges. Bake until golden brown and tester inserted into center comes out clean, about 25 minutes. Cool slightly. Recut into 8 wedges.

Green Chili Corn Bread

12 servings

¾ cup (1½ sticks) unsalted butter, room temperature
1 cup yellow cornmeal
6 tablespoons sugar
4 large eggs
1½ cups all purpose flour
1 tablespoon baking powder

1½ teaspoons salt
1 15-ounce can cream-style corn
1 4-ounce can diced green chilies
⅓ cup (packed) grated cheddar cheese (about 1½ ounces)
⅓ cup (packed) grated Monterey Jack cheese (about 1½ ounces)

Preheat oven to 375°F. Lightly oil 9-inch square baking pan. Using electric mixer, beat butter, cornmeal and sugar in large bowl until well blended. Add eggs 1 at a time, beating well after each addition. Mix flour, baking powder and salt in small bowl. Add to batter and stir well. Mix in corn, chilies and both cheeses. Pour batter into prepared pan. Bake until tester inserted into center comes out clean, about 45 minutes. Cool slightly. Cut into squares.

Raspberry Bran Muffins

Makes about 24

2½ cups all purpose flour
1¾ cups sugar
2 teaspoons baking powder
½ teaspoon baking soda
½ teaspoon salt

2 cups buttermilk
½ cup vegetable oil
2 large eggs
8 cups bran flakes cereal
½ cup raspberry jam

Preheat oven to 350°F. Line muffin tins with paper muffin cups. Combine first 5 ingredients in medium bowl. Whisk buttermilk, oil and eggs in large bowl to blend. Add dry ingredients and cereal and stir until just blended. Spoon ¼ cup batter into each muffin cup. Using small spoon, make well in center of each and fill well with 1 teaspoon jam. Spoon remaining batter over. Bake until tester inserted into centers comes out clean, about 25 minutes. Turn muffins out onto racks. Cool slightly. Serve warm or at room temperature.

French Bread with Goat Cheese and Sun-dried Tomato Spread

8 servings

1 11-ounce package soft fresh goat cheese (such as Montrachet)
⅔ cup chopped walnuts
½ cup chopped drained oil-packed sun-dried tomatoes
4 teaspoons minced fresh thyme or 1 teaspoon dried, crumbled
¼ cup (about) sour cream

Minced fresh thyme
Chopped walnuts
2 French bread baguettes, sliced

Mix first 4 ingredients in bowl. Thin to spreadable consistency with sour cream. Season with generous amount of pepper. Mound cheese in crock or bowl. (*Can be prepared up to 2 days ahead. Cover and refrigerate. Bring cheese to room temperature before serving.*)
Sprinkle cheese with thyme and walnuts. Serve with bread.

6 ❦ Desserts

At *Bon Appétit*, we like to think of desserts as one of our strong suits, one of the things we do best. We run at least one dessert story every month, and feature sweets of all kinds throughout the magazine. All of which made it very difficult to choose our favorites among the hundreds that ran during the twelve months of 1992. We managed, though, narrowing it down to the fifty-five recipes you'll find here, each one of them a winner in its own right.

No matter the season, fruit desserts always seem appropriate, whether you're serving a warming cobbler in the winter, say Cherry Cobbler with Rum Whipped Cream, or a light poached-fruit dessert, maybe Poached Peaches with Vanilla, in the summer. And while frozen desserts make ideal hot-weather treats, there are some here that may become year-round favorites, including Frozen Strawberry-Banana Cake with Strawberry Sauce and snack-perfect Nut and Chip Burgers.

Pies, tarts and cakes are stylish endings to any meal, and it's likely there's one here for every occasion you can imagine. Fudge-Pecan Pie would be just right after a southern feast of fried chicken, mashed potatoes and biscuits, while the Ginger, Coconut and Papaya Tart would end an Asian meal on a deliciously sweet note. To celebrate a chocolate lover's birthday, how about the Triple-Layer Devil's Food Cake, covered in a bittersweet chocolate frosting and decorated with white chocolate and milk chocolate shavings?

Sometimes the perfect dessert is just a bite or two of something sweet. Cookies and brownies fill that bill. Among the offerings here are Spiced Molasses Ginger Cookies, Rocky Road Wedges, White Chocolate Chunk Brownies and Lemon Pudding Cookies.

🍎 *Fruit Desserts*

Apple-Blackberry Crisp

12 servings

Topping
2 cups all purpose flour
1½ cups sugar
¼ teaspoon salt
1 cup (2 sticks) chilled unsalted
butter, cut into pieces

Fruit
5 pounds Golden Delicious apples,
peeled, cored, thinly sliced
1½ cups fresh blackberries or frozen,
thawed, drained
1 cup sugar
¼ cup all purpose flour

For topping: Mix flour, sugar and salt in processor. Add butter and blend in using on/off turns until mixture resembles coarse crumbs. (*Can be prepared 1 day ahead. Cover and refrigerate.*)

For fruit: Preheat oven to 350°F. Butter 9 × 13-inch baking dish. Toss apples, blackberries, sugar and flour in large bowl. Transfer mixture to prepared baking dish, mounding slightly.

Crumble topping over fruit. Bake until fruit bubbles and topping is golden brown, about 1 hour. Cool at least 15 minutes. Scoop into bowls and serve warm.

Baked Peaches with Cointreau

6 servings

⅓ cup peach nectar
6 peaches, peeled, halved, pitted
3 tablespoons brown sugar
⅓ cup Cointreau or other orange
liqueur

3 tablespoons chilled unsalted
butter, cut into small pieces

Vanilla ice cream or frozen
yogurt
Additional Cointreau or other
orange liqueur (optional)

Preheat oven to 375°F. Generously butter 9-inch square baking dish. Pour nectar into prepared dish. Arrange peaches cut side up in dish. Sprinkle with sugar. Drizzle Cointreau over. Top with butter. Bake until peaches are tender, about 30 minutes. Let cool 10 minutes.

Scoop ice cream into bowls. Top with peaches; spoon juices from dish over. Serve, passing additional Cointreau separately if desired.

🍎

Pears Poached in Spiced Red Wine with Bow-Tie Pastries

6 servings

Pears

1 750-ml bottle dry red wine
1 cup water
1 cup sugar
4 whole cloves
4 2 × 1-inch lemon peel strips
1 vanilla bean, split lengthwise
6 firm ripe pears, peeled
¼ cup plus 1 tablespoon anisette

Pastries

1 cup all purpose flour
3 tablespoons powdered sugar

1 tablespoon aniseed, chopped
1 tablespoon (generous) minced lemon peel (yellow part only)
¼ cup milk
3 tablespoons unsalted butter, melted
½ teaspoon vanilla extract

Vegetable oil (for deep frying)
Powdered sugar

Vanilla ice cream

For pears: Combine first 5 ingredients in heavy large saucepan. Scrape in seeds from vanilla bean; add bean. Bring to boil, stirring to dissolve sugar. Add pears, reduce heat, cover and simmer until pears are tender when pierced with knife, about 20 minutes. Stir in ¼ cup anisette. Cool pears completely in syrup. Cover; refrigerate in syrup overnight.

Transfer pears to medium bowl. Cover and refrigerate pears. Boil poaching liquid in heavy large saucepan until reduced to 1 cup, about 35 minutes. Mix in remaining 1 tablespoon anisette. Cover and refrigerate liquid until cold, 4 hours.

For pastries: Mix flour, 3 tablespoons sugar, aniseed and lemon peel in large bowl. Add milk, butter and vanilla and stir until dough forms. Cover dough with plastic wrap and let stand 30 minutes at room temperature.

Roll dough out on lightly floured surface to thickness of 1/16 inch. Cut dough into 3½ × ¾-inch strips. Trim ends diagonally. Twist strips at center to create bow ties. (*Can be prepared 1 day ahead. Place bow ties on cookie sheet. Cover tightly and refrigerate.*)

Line cookie sheet with paper towels. Heat 2 inches oil in heavy medium saucepan to 375°F. Add 4 bow-tie pastries and cook until deep golden brown, turning occasionally, about 1 minute. Transfer to paper towels using slotted spoon. Repeat with remaining pastries in batches. Place sugar in large bowl. Add warm pastries and toss to coat.

Arrange pears on plates. Place scoop of ice cream on 1 side of each plate. Drizzle poaching liquid over pears. Garnish with pastries and serve.

Grand Fruit Salad

8 servings

2 cups green grapes
2 cups sliced strawberries
2 cups sliced plums
1 cup sliced peaches
1 cup orange segments

1 cup sliced peeled kiwi fruit
½ cup Grand Marnier or other orange liqueur
½ cup orange juice
2 tablespoons sugar

Combine all ingredients in large bowl. Cover and refrigerate up to 8 hours.

Cherry Cobbler with Rum Whipped Cream

6 servings

Filling
4 cups pitted tart cherries or
1 20-ounce bag frozen pitted
cherries, thawed
¾ cup sugar
2 tablespoons cornstarch
1 tablespoon fresh lemon juice
1½ teaspoons grated lemon peel
½ teaspoon ground cinnamon
¼ teaspoon ground nutmeg
3 tablespoons unsalted butter, cut
into pieces

Cobbler Topping
1 cup all purpose flour
¼ cup sugar

1½ teaspoons baking powder
½ teaspoon salt
2 tablespoons (¼ stick) chilled
unsalted butter, cut into pieces
⅔ cup whipping cream

1 tablespoon butter, melted
2 tablespoons sugar

Whipped Cream
½ cup crème fraîche or sour cream
¼ cup packed golden brown sugar
1 cup chilled whipping cream
2 tablespoons dark rum

For filling: Preheat oven to 400°F. Butter 9-inch round baking dish. Combine first 7 ingredients in bowl. Pour into prepared dish. Dot with butter. Set aside.

For cobbler topping: Combine first 4 ingredients in medium bowl. Add 2 tablespoons chilled butter and cut in until coarse meal forms. Add whipping cream and stir until soft dough forms. Roll dough out on lightly floured surface to 6-inch square. Cut dough into twelve 2 × 1½-inch rectangles.

Arrange dough rectangles side by side atop cherry filling in dish. Brush dough with 1 tablespoon melted butter and sprinkle with sugar. Bake until biscuits are puffed and golden brown, about 30 minutes. Cool cobbler slightly.

For whipped cream: Mix crème fraîche and sugar in large bowl until sugar dissolves. Add cream and rum and beat until soft peaks form.

Serve cobbler warm with whipped cream.

Poached Peaches with Vanilla

A sophisticated dessert that is great on its own, mixed with sweet berries or used as a topping for ice cream or frozen yogurt.

4 servings

1 cup semisweet white wine (such
as French Colombard)
½ cup water
⅓ cup sugar
2 tablespoons honey

1 vanilla bean, split lengthwise
1¼ pounds firm ripe peaches
(unpeeled), cut into ½-inch-thick
slices

Bring first 5 ingredients to simmer in heavy medium saucepan, stirring to dissolve sugar. Remove from heat. Scrape seeds from vanilla bean into syrup. Return bean to syrup. Cover and continue simmering 5 minutes. Add peaches and poach until just tender when pierced with tip of sharp knife, about 4 minutes. Transfer mixture to bowl and refrigerate until cold, at least 3 hours. (*Can be prepared up to 3 days ahead.*)

Remove vanilla bean and any loose pieces of peach skin before serving.

Blackberry-Nectarine Crisp

12 servings

Topping

1¼ cups old-fashioned oats
1 cup plus 2 tablespoons firmly
   packed brown sugar
¾ cup all purpose flour
1 tablespoon grated lemon peel
¾ cup (1½ sticks) unsalted butter

Fruit

3 pounds nectarines, halved, pitted,
   cut into ½-inch-wide wedges
6 cups fresh blackberries or frozen
   unsweetened, thawed, drained
1½ cups sugar
2 tablespoons instant tapioca

Vanilla ice cream or frozen
yogurt

For topping: Combine first 4 ingredients in processor. Add butter and cut in using on/off turns until mixture resembles coarse meal. (*Topping can be prepared up to 1 day ahead. Cover and refrigerate.*)

For fruit: Preheat oven to 375°F. Toss nectarines, berries, sugar and tapioca in large bowl. Let stand 15 minutes.

Transfer fruit mixture to 9 × 13-inch baking dish. Sprinkle topping over. Bake until topping browns and fruit bubbles, about 50 minutes. Cool slightly. Spoon crisp into bowls. Top with ice cream.

🍒 Custards, Puddings and Mousses

Raspberry Crème Brûlée

Cooking the custard on the stove (instead of baking it) is what produces a very soft and creamy texture.

6 servings

12 ounces frozen unsweetened
   raspberries, thawed, drained
¾ cup sugar
2 teaspoons raspberry liqueur
   (optional)
5 egg yolks

2 cups whipping cream
¼ teaspoon vanilla extract
5 tablespoons unsalted butter

⅓ cup firmly packed brown sugar

Gently toss berries with ¼ cup sugar and liqueur in bowl. Divide berries among six ¾-cup broilerproof ramekins or custard cups. Whisk egg yolks and remaining ½ cup sugar in heavy medium saucepan until pale and thick, about 3 minutes. Add cream and vanilla. Set saucepan over medium heat and stir until custard thickens and leaves path on back of spoon when finger is drawn across, about 7 minutes; do not boil. Add butter and stir until melted. Carefully spoon over berries. Cover and refrigerate at least 4 hours or overnight.

Preheat broiler. Press brown sugar through sieve over custards. Broil until sugar begins to melt and caramelize, about 2 minutes. Chill 3 hours.

Pistachio Soufflé with Chocolate Sorbet

4 servings

Sorbet
2 cups plus 2 tablespoons water
1 cup unsweetened cocoa powder
⅔ cup sugar
3 ounces bittersweet (not unsweetened) or semisweet chocolate, chopped

Soufflé
2 cups plus 2 tablespoons milk
2 cups shelled unsalted pistachio nuts, toasted, chopped
1 vanilla bean, split lengthwise

3 large egg yolks
½ cup sugar
2 tablespoons all purpose flour
¼ teaspoon almond extract

4 large egg whites

For sorbet: Combine 2 cups plus 2 tablespoons water, cocoa powder, sugar and chocolate in heavy medium saucepan. Bring to boil, whisking constantly. Strain into bowl. Refrigerate for 1 hour.

Transfer chocolate mixture to ice cream maker and process according to manufacturer's instructions. Freeze in covered container until firm. (*Sorbet can be prepared up to 2 days ahead.*)

For soufflé: Bring milk and nuts to boil in heavy medium saucepan. Add vanilla bean. Remove from heat, cover and let stand 20 minutes.

Strain milk mixture into medium bowl, pressing on solids with back of spoon. Scrape seeds from vanilla bean into strained milk mixture. Beat egg yolks, ¼ cup sugar and flour in another medium bowl. Gradually whisk in milk mixture. Return milk mixture to saucepan. Bring to boil, whisking constantly. Boil until thickened, about 1 minute. Strain pastry cream into bowl. Stir in almond extract. Place plastic wrap directly on surface of pastry cream. Refrigerate until well chilled, about 4 hours. (*Can be prepared 2 days ahead.*)

Preheat oven to 350°F. Butter four 1-cup soufflé dishes or custard cups. Dust with sugar. Beat egg whites in large bowl to soft peaks. Gradually add remaining ¼ cup sugar and beat to stiff peaks. Fold whites into pastry cream. Divide mixture among prepared dishes. Bake until golden and well puffed above rims, about 30 minutes. Top each with scoop of sorbet and serve.

Lemon Custard

The custard separates as it bakes, forming two layers.

4 servings

1 cup sugar
½ cup fresh lemon juice
3 large eggs
3 large egg yolks
½ cup whipping cream

Lemon slices
Fresh mint sprigs

Preheat oven to 325°F. Whisk 1 cup sugar, ½ cup fresh lemon juice, eggs and egg yolks in large bowl until well blended. Gradually whisk in whipping cream. Strain through sieve into four ¾-cup custard cups. Arrange cups in baking pan.

Add enough hot water to baking pan to come halfway up sides of custard cups. Bake until custards are barely set in center, about 30 minutes. Remove cups from water and cool slightly. Cover and refrigerate overnight. (*Can be prepared up to 2 days ahead; keep refrigerated.*)

Run small sharp knife around custards to loosen. Turn custards out onto plates. Garnish custards with lemon slices and fresh mint sprigs.

Pumpkin and Bran Bread Pudding

10 servings

2 cups half and half
6 large eggs
1 cup sugar
1 cup canned solid-pack pumpkin
1 tablespoon vanilla extract
2 teaspoons ground cinnamon
1 teaspoon ground nutmeg

7½ cups ¾-inch pieces purchased bran muffins (about 10 muffins)
1 cup chopped toasted pecans (about 4 ounces)
Vanilla ice cream
Honey

Preheat oven to 350°F. Butter 9 × 13 × 2-inch glass baking dish. Whisk first 7 ingredients in large bowl. Add muffins and pecans and stir to combine. Pour mixture into prepared dish. Bake until tester inserted into center comes out clean, about 45 minutes. Cool slightly. Spoon pudding into bowls. Top with ice cream. Drizzle with honey and serve.

Rice Pudding with Cream Sherry

4 servings

6 cups (about) milk
1 cup short- or medium-grain white rice
½ cup sugar
2 cinnamon sticks
1 vanilla bean (split lengthwise)

¼ teaspoon salt
½ cup cream Sherry
½ cup firmly packed brown sugar

Additional brown sugar

Combine 5 cups milk, rice, ½ cup sugar, cinnamon, vanilla and salt in heavy medium saucepan. Bring to boil. Reduce heat to low and cook until rice is tender and mixture is thick, stirring frequently, about 50 minutes. Mix in cream Sherry and ½ cup packed brown sugar.

Serve pudding hot or well chilled. Thin with milk if pudding is too thick. Spoon into bowls. Press additional brown sugar through sieve atop puddings.

Classic Flan

6 servings

1¾ cups whipping cream
1 cup milk (do not use low-fat or nonfat)
Pinch of salt
½ vanilla bean, split lengthwise

1 cup sugar
⅓ cup water

3 large eggs
2 large egg yolks
7 tablespoons sugar

Position rack in center of oven and preheat to 350°F. Combine cream, milk and salt in heavy medium saucepan. Scrape seeds from vanilla bean into cream mixture; add bean. Bring to simmer over medium heat. Remove cream mixture from heat and let steep 30 minutes.

Meanwhile, combine 1 cup sugar and ⅓ cup water in another heavy medium saucepan. Stir over low heat until sugar dissolves. Increase heat to high and cook without stirring until syrup turns deep amber, brushing down sides of pan with wet pastry brush and swirling pan occasionally, about 10 minutes. Quickly pour caramel into six ¾-cup ramekins or custard cups. Using oven mitts as aid, immediately tilt each ramekin to coat sides. Set ramekins into 13 × 9 × 2-inch baking pan. Set aside.

Whisk eggs, egg yolks and 7 tablespoons sugar in medium bowl just until blended. Gradually and gently whisk cream mixture into egg mixture without creating lots of foam. Pour custard through small sieve into prepared ramekins, dividing evenly (mixture will fill ramekins). Pour enough hot water into baking pan to come halfway up sides of ramekins.

Bake until centers of flans are gently set, about 40 minutes. Transfer flans to rack and cool. Chill until cold, about 2 hours. Cover and refrigerate overnight. (*Can be prepared up to 2 days ahead.*)

To serve, run small sharp knife around flan to loosen. Turn over onto plate. Shake gently to release flan. Carefully lift off ramekin allowing caramel syrup to run over flan. Repeat with remaining flans and serve.

❦ Frozen Desserts

Peanut Butter and Chocolate Sorbet Sandwiches

A modern take on old-fashioned ice cream sandwiches and ice cream cone "drumsticks."

Makes 6 sandwiches

2 cups water
¾ cup sugar
¾ cup unsweetened cocoa powder (preferably Dutch process)
¼ cup light corn syrup
4 peanut butter cup candies (about 3.2 ounces total), cut into ¼-inch pieces

12 Pepperidge Farm Cheyenne cookies (peanut butter chunk)

6 ounces semisweet chocolate, chopped
1¼ cups chopped roasted unsalted peanuts

Whisk first 4 ingredients in heavy medium saucepan over medium heat until sugar dissolves. Increase heat and bring to boil, whisking frequently. Pour into bowl. Chill until cold. Transfer to ice cream maker and process according to manufacturer's instructions. Transfer sorbet to container; mix in peanut butter candies. Freeze sorbet overnight.

Line cookie sheet with foil. Sandwich ⅓ cup sorbet between flat sides of 2 cookies, pressing slightly to bring sorbet to edge of sandwich; smooth sides. Place on cookie sheet and freeze. Repeat with remaining sorbet and cookies. Freeze until firm, at least 3 hours.

Melt chocolate in top of double boiler over simmering water, stirring until smooth. Remove from over water. Working quickly, roll sides of sandwich in warm chocolate, turning to coat sides only. Roll coated sides in chopped nuts. Return sandwich to same cookie sheet. Repeat with remaining sandwiches, melted chocolate and chopped nuts. Freeze until firm, about 1 hour. (*Can be prepared 1 week ahead. Wrap tightly.*)

❦

Frozen Strawberry-Banana Cake with Strawberry Sauce

Purchased sorbet, frozen yogurt and pound cake make this a quick and elegant dessert.

12 servings

1 12-ounce pound cake
1 cup strawberry preserves
¼ cup strawberry liqueur or orange juice
2 pints strawberry sorbet, softened
2 pints banana-strawberry frozen yogurt, softened

1 10-ounce package frozen sliced strawberries in syrup, thawed
3 large ripe bananas, peeled, cut diagonally into ¼-inch-thick slices
Sliced fresh strawberries

Cut cake into ¼-inch-thick slices. Arrange enough slices in bottom of 9-inch-diameter springform pan with 2¾-inch-high sides to just cover bottom, fitting tightly. Cook preserves and liqueur in heavy small saucepan over medium heat until reduced to ⅔ cup, stirring frequently, about 14 minutes. Spread half of preserves mixture over cake in pan. Freeze 10 minutes. Spoon sorbet over cake in pan; smooth top. Arrange more cake slices over to just cover sorbet. Spread remaining preserves mixture over cake. Freeze 10 minutes.

Spoon frozen yogurt over cake; smooth top. Cover and freeze overnight. (*Can be prepared up to 1 week ahead.*)

Puree thawed berries in processor. Cover and refrigerate until cold. (*Sauce can be prepared up to 2 days ahead.*)

Release pan sides from cake. Place banana slices around cake edge. Mound berries in center. Serve cake with sauce.

Mint Chocolate Ice Cream Cake

8 servings

1 16-ounce package chocolate sandwich cookies
3 tablespoons unsalted butter, melted

1 quart mint chocolate chip ice cream

1 quart cookies and cream ice cream
1 10-ounce package mint chocolate chips

Finely grind cookies in processor. Blend in melted butter. Press crumb mixture evenly onto bottom and 2¼ inches up sides of 9 × 2¾-inch springform pan. Refrigerate crust for 30 minutes.

Meanwhile, soften mint ice cream slightly, about 2 minutes in microwave set on medium-low or in refrigerator. Spread mint ice cream evenly in chilled crust. Freeze until set but not solid, about 1 hour.

Soften cookies and cream ice cream. Spread evenly over mint ice cream in pan. Freeze at least 2 hours or overnight. Melt chocolate chips in top of double boiler over simmering water, stirring until smooth. Using fork, lightly drizzle some chocolate back and forth over cake, creating design. Release sides of pan. Cut cake into wedges. Serve cake immediately, passing remaining melted chocolate chips separately as sauce.

Sunset Sorbet Sundaes

Colorful boysenberry and mango sorbets team up in a refreshing, guilt-free alternative to traditional ice cream sundaes.

6 servings

1 16-ounce bag frozen unsweetened boysenberries or blackberries, thawed
½ cup plus 6 tablespoons sugar
½ cup light corn syrup
¼ cup water
¼ cup crème de cassis (optional)

2 large mangoes, peeled, pitted
1 mango, peeled, pitted, sliced
1 1-pint basket fresh boysenberries or blackberries

Combine thawed boysenberries, ½ cup sugar, ¼ cup corn syrup, ¼ cup water and crème de cassis in heavy medium saucepan. Bring to simmer, stirring frequently. Puree in processor. Strain into medium bowl, pressing on solids with spoon. Pour ¾ cup puree into small bowl; cover and refrigerate to use later as sauce. Refrigerate remaining berry puree in medium bowl until cold. Transfer puree in medium bowl to ice cream maker and process according to manufacturer's instructions. Transfer sorbet to container and freeze.

Puree 2 mangoes in processor. Measure puree and return 1⅔ cups to processor. Reserve any remaining puree for another use. Add remaining 6 tablespoons sugar and remaining ¼ cup corn syrup to processor; blend well. Transfer mango puree to ice cream maker and freeze according to manufacturer's instructions. Transfer sorbet to container and freeze. (*Sauce and sorbets can be prepared up to 2 days ahead.*)

Scoop sorbets into parfait dishes or onto plates. Garnish with sliced mango and berries. Spoon sauce over and serve.

Sundaes with Chocolate, Caramel and Macadamia Nut Sauce

4 servings

1¼ cups sugar
⅓ cup bourbon or water
¾ cup whipping cream
3 tablespoons unsalted butter

1½ ounces bittersweet (not unsweetened) or semisweet chocolate, chopped
1 cup macadamia nuts

Vanilla ice cream

Stir sugar and bourbon in heavy medium saucepan over low heat until sugar dissolves. Increase heat to medium-high. Boil without stirring until mixture turns deep amber color, brushing down sides of pan with wet pastry brush and swirling pan occasionally, about 8 minutes. Remove from heat. Add cream (mixture will bubble up) and whisk until smooth. Return to boil, whisking constantly. Remove from heat, add butter and chocolate and stir until smooth. Mix in nuts. (*Can be made 1 week ahead. Cover and chill. Before using, rewarm over low heat, stirring and thinning with small amount of water if necessary.*)

Top scoops of ice cream with sauce and serve.

Pera Bella Helena

This dessert is an Italian takeoff on a classic French dish, Poire Belle-Hélène—poached pear with vanilla ice cream and chocolate sauce. Here the pear is teamed with a hazelnut-orange semifreddo (a sweet Italian frozen mousse) and a Frangelico chocolate sauce. For smaller appetites, cut the semifreddo into eight portions and the poached pears in half.

4 servings

Semifreddo
- ¾ cup chilled whipping cream
- 1 pint vanilla ice cream, slightly softened
- ½ cup chopped husked toasted hazelnuts
- 3 tablespoons Frangelico or other nut liqueur
- 1 ounce bittersweet (not unsweetened) or semisweet chocolate, finely grated
- ½ teaspoon grated orange peel

Sauce
- ¼ cup whipping cream
- ¼ cup Frangelico liqueur
- Pinch of salt
- 6 ounces bittersweet (not unsweetened) or semisweet chocolate, chopped
- ¼ cup light corn syrup

Pears
- 6 cups water
- 1½ cups sugar
- 8 1 × 3-inch orange peel strips
- 2 teaspoons vanilla extract
- 4 small firm ripe Anjou, Bartlett or Comice pears, peeled

- ¼ cup chopped husked toasted hazelnuts
- 4 orange slices

For semifreddo: Line 8-inch square pan with plastic. Whip ¾ cup cream to soft peaks in medium bowl. Mix ice cream, hazelnuts, liqueur, chocolate and orange peel in large bowl just until blended. Gently fold in whipped cream. Transfer mixture to prepared pan; smooth top. Cover and freeze until firm, at least 4 hours. (*Can be prepared 4 days ahead. Keep frozen.*)

For sauce: Bring cream, liqueur and salt to boil in heavy small saucepan. Remove from heat and add chocolate. Let stand 3 minutes. Whisk until chocolate is melted and sauce is smooth. Whisk in corn syrup. (*Can be prepared 3 days ahead. Cover and refrigerate.*)

For pears: Stir first 4 ingredients in heavy medium saucepan over medium heat until sugar dissolves. Bring to boil. Reduce heat, add pears and simmer until pears are just tender, about 20 minutes. Remove pears from poaching liquid. Cool pears and syrup separately. Return pears to syrup and refrigerate until cold. (*Can be prepared 8 hours ahead.*)

Stir chocolate sauce over low heat until warm. Cut semifreddo into 4 squares. Place 1 semifreddo piece in each of 4 bowls. Remove pears from syrup with slotted spoon. Place pears atop semifreddo. Spoon chocolate sauce over pears to coat, letting extra sauce drizzle onto semifreddo and plate. Sprinkle with nuts. Garnish with orange slices and serve.

Coffee and Orange Granita Suprema

You don't need an ice cream maker to prepare this classic frozen treat. Accompany with amaretti or other Italian cookies.

6 servings

- 4 cups hot espresso or strong coffee made with ground espresso coffee beans
- ½ cup sugar
- 1 teaspoon grated orange peel
- ⅛ teaspoon ground cinnamon
- ¾ cup well-chilled whipping cream
- 3 tablespoons sugar
- 2 tablespoons Grand Marnier or other orange liqueur
- Milk chocolate curls
- Thin orange peel strips

Mix coffee, ½ cup sugar, grated orange peel and ground cinnamon in medium bowl until sugar dissolves. Cool to room temperature. Transfer mixture to loaf

Musician's Tart

Classic Flan

Henry Hamamoto

Salmon with Arugula, Tomato and Caper Sauce; Pasta with Sugar Snap Peas, Asparagus and Parmesan

Lannen/Kelly

Sunshine Cheesecake

Chicken Tajine with Vegetable Couscous

Pear and Pine Nut Frangipane Tartlets; Pera Bella Helena;
Brandied Pear and Currant Strudel with Brandy Custard Sauce

Joel Lipton

Fontina, Mushroom and Pancetta Lasagna

David Bishop

pan. Freeze until granita is consistency of shaved ice, stirring mixture with fork and breaking up frozen edge pieces every 30 minutes, about 3 hours. (*Granita can be made 6 hours ahead. If possible, stir every 30 minutes to 1 hour. Before serving, blend mixture in processor to break up ice.*)

Beat chilled whipping cream and 3 tablespoons sugar in medium bowl until soft peaks form. Add Grand Marnier and beat until soft peaks form again. Spoon granita into bowls. Top each dessert with dollop of whipped cream. Garnish with chocolate curls and orange peel strips and serve immediately.

Nut and Chip Burgers

Makes 6 ice cream sandwiches

½ cup (1 stick) unsalted butter, room temperature
½ cup firmly packed dark brown sugar
6 tablespoons sugar
1 large egg
½ teaspoon vanilla extract
1 cup plus 2 tablespoons all purpose flour

½ teaspoon baking soda
Pinch of salt
1 cup white chocolate chips
1 cup chopped toasted hazelnuts (about 4 ounces)

Additional sugar

1 pint vanilla ice cream, softened

Preheat oven to 350°F. Line 2 large cookie sheets with parchment. Using electric mixer, beat first 3 ingredients in large bowl until well blended. Add egg and vanilla and blend well. Mix flour, baking soda and salt in small bowl. Add to butter mixture and stir to combine. Mix in chocolate chips and hazelnuts.

Drop dough by scant ⅓ cupfuls onto prepared cookie sheets, spacing evenly and forming 12 mounds total. Dip bottom of glass in sugar and press on 1 mound of dough to flatten to ½-inch-thick round. Repeat with remaining dough mounds, dipping glass into sugar for each. Bake until cookies are golden brown, about 15 minutes. Cool cookies on sheets 2 minutes. Transfer cookies to rack and cool completely. (*Can be prepared 2 days ahead. Store in airtight container at room temperature.*)

Place cookies in freezer 10 minutes. Spoon ⅓ cup ice cream onto flat side of 1 cookie. Top with flat side of second cookie, pressing to push ice cream to cookie edge. Place in freezer. Repeat with remaining cookies and ice cream. Freeze until firm, about 1 hour. (*Can be prepared up to 1 week ahead. Wrap sandwiches tightly in plasic and freeze.*)

❦ *Pies, Tarts and Pastries*

Brandied Pear and Currant Strudel with Brandy Custard Sauce

6 servings

⅔ cup dried currants
⅓ cup brandy
⅓ cup water

1¾ pounds firm ripe pears, peeled, cored, diced (about 4 generous cups)
½ cup sugar
¼ cup brandy
3 tablespoons water
2 tablespoons cornstarch

½ cup plus 2 tablespoons (1¼ sticks) unsalted butter, melted, cooled
14 vanilla wafer cookies
½ cup toasted walnuts
9 frozen phyllo pastry sheets, thawed

Fresh currants or grape clusters (optional)
Brandy Custard Sauce (see recipe)

Simmer first 3 ingredients in heavy 10-inch skillet over low heat until mixture appears dry, approximately 5 minutes.

Toss pears, sugar, ¼ cup brandy, 3 tablespoons water and cornstarch to combine in large bowl. Add to skillet with currants and cook over medium heat until pears are tender and mixture is very thick, stirring occasionally, about 18 minutes. Cover and cool completely. (*Filling can be prepared 1 day ahead. Cover with plastic and refrigerate.*)

Brush heavy large cookie sheet with some of melted butter. Finely grind vanilla wafers and walnuts in processor. Place towel on work surface. Place 1 phyllo sheet on towel. (Keep remaining phyllo covered with plastic and damp towel.) Brush with butter. Top with second phyllo sheet. Brush with butter and sprinkle with 3 tablespoons cookie crumb mixture. Repeat layering phyllo, butter and crumbs 5 more times, sprinkling each layer with crumbs. Top with remaining 2 phyllo sheets, buttering each. Spoon filling in 3½-inch-wide log down 1 long side of phyllo, 2 inches in from edge and leaving 2-inch border at each end. Fold short sides over filling. Using towel as aid, carefully roll up strudel jelly roll style. Transfer to prepared cookie sheet, seam side down. Brush with butter. (*Strudel can be prepared up to 4 hours ahead. Cover tightly with plastic wrap, then towel; refrigerate.*)

Position rack in center of oven and preheat to 375°F. Carefully slice through top few sheets of phyllo (do not cut through to filling), marking strudel into 6 equal pieces. Bake until golden brown, about 45 minutes. Cool at least 10 minutes. Cut through strudel at marked sections. Place 1 piece of strudel on each of 6 plates. Garnish with fresh currants or grapes. Pass sauce separately.

❦

Brandy Custard Sauce

Makes about 1¾ cups

¼ cup brandy
1¼ cups whipping cream
4 egg yolks

¼ cup sugar
1 teaspoon vanilla extract

Boil brandy in heavy small saucepan until reduced to 2 tablespoons, about 1 minute. Add cream and return to boil. Beat yolks with sugar in bowl to blend. Gradually whisk hot cream mixture into yolks. Return mixture to saucepan. Stir over low heat until sauce thickens and leaves path on back of spoon when finger is drawn across, about 3 minutes; do not boil. Pour sauce into bowl; mix in vanilla. Refrigerate. (*Can be prepared 1 day ahead. Cover and chill.*)

Triple Berry Tart (Cover Recipe)

Blackberries, strawberries and blueberries are used here, but any trio of fresh seasonal berries will do.

6 servings

Crust
1¾ cups all purpose flour
⅓ cup sugar
1 tablespoon grated lemon peel
½ teaspoon salt
¾ cup (1½ sticks) chilled unsalted butter, cut into pieces
2 large egg yolks
1 tablespoon fresh lemon juice
1 teaspoon vanilla extract
1 tablespoon (about) water

Filling
⅓ cup red currant jelly
¼ cup raspberry jam
2 tablespoons framboise eau-de-vie (clear raspberry brandy), kirsch (clear cherry brandy) or orange juice
1 ½-pint basket blackberries or boysenberries
1 1-pint basket strawberries, hulled
½ cup (about) fresh blueberries

For crust: Mix flour, sugar, lemon peel and salt in large bowl. Add butter pieces and blend in using fingertips until mixture resembles coarse meal. Whisk egg yolks, lemon juice and vanilla extract in small bowl to blend. Add to flour mixture and stir until moist clumps form, adding water by tablespoons if mixture is dry. Gather dough into ball and flatten into disk. Wrap dough tightly in plastic and refrigerate 3 hours.

Roll dough out on lightly floured surface to 13-inch round. Transfer dough to 9-inch-diameter tart pan with removable bottom. Press dough onto bottom and up sides; trim edges. Pierce bottom with fork. Refrigerate 2 hours.

Preheat oven to 425°F. Line crust with aluminum foil. Fill crust with dried beans or pie weights. Bake crust 10 minutes. Remove foil and beans. Bake crust until golden brown, about 20 minutes more. Transfer to rack and cool.

For filling: Cook red currant jelly, raspberry jam and brandy in heavy small saucepan over medium-high heat until thick, stirring frequently, about 3 minutes. Brush some of jam glaze over bottom of tart. Arrange circle of blackberries in ring around inside of tart edge. Arrange strawberries in ring, pointed ends up, inside ring of blackberries. Fill center of tart with blueberries. Brush more jam glaze over all berries. (*Tart can be prepared 2 hours ahead. Let stand at room temperature.*) Cut into wedges and serve.

Fruit and Nut Tart

6 servings

Crust
1¼ cups all purpose flour
3 tablespoons sugar
Pinch of salt
½ cup (1 stick) chilled unsalted butter, cut into pieces
1 egg yolk
½ teaspoon vanilla extract
6 teaspoons (about) whipping cream

Fruit Filling
1 cup (scant) dried pears, cored, coarsely chopped (4 ounces)
1 cup (scant) pitted dates, halved
⅓ cup pear nectar
¼ cup firmly packed dark brown sugar

Nut Topping
6 tablespoons (¾ stick) unsalted butter
6 tablespoons firmly packed dark brown sugar
3 tablespoons light corn syrup
½ cup pine nuts (about 2 ounces)
½ cup toasted whole almonds (about 2 ounces)
½ cup dry roasted cashew nuts (about 2 ounces)
1½ tablespoons whipping cream

For crust: Mix first 3 ingredients in processor. Add butter and cut in using on/off turns until mixture resembles coarse meal. Blend in yolk and vanilla using on/off turns. Blend in enough cream by teaspoonfuls to form dough that begins to clump together. Gather dough into ball; flatten into disk. Wrap dough in plastic and refrigerate for 30 minutes.

Preheat oven to 350°F. Roll out dough between sheets of waxed paper to 12-inch round. Transfer dough to 9-inch-diameter tart pan with removable bottom. Trim edges. Freeze crust 15 minutes. Line with foil. Fill with dried beans or pie weights. Bake until sides are set, about 10 minutes. Remove foil and beans; bake crust until golden, about 20 minutes more. Cool completely on rack.

For fruit filling: Combine all ingredients in heavy medium saucepan and bring to boil. Reduce heat and simmer 1 minute. Puree mixture in processor to thick paste. Cool fruit filling completely.

For nut topping: Preheat oven to 400°F. Cook first 3 ingredients in heavy large saucepan over low heat, stirring until sugar dissolves. Increase heat and bring to boil. Boil vigorously 1 minute. Remove from heat. Add nuts and cream.

Spread fruit filling in crust; smooth top. Set tart on cookie sheet. Spoon nut topping over. Bake until filling bubbles, about 20 minutes. Transfer tart to rack and cool 10 minutes. Using oven mitts, loosen tart pan sides but do not remove. Cool tart completely in pan. (*Can be prepared 1 day ahead. Cover and let stand at room temperature.*) Remove pan sides. Cut tart into wedges.

Peach-Frangipane Tart

*Sophisticated and simple—
even more so with the help
of a purchased pie crust.*

6 servings

1 **All Ready Pie Crust (half of
15-ounce package), room
temperature**
2 **tablespoons all purpose flour**
¾ **cup slivered blanched almonds
(about 3½ ounces)**
⅓ **cup sugar**

3 **tablespoons amaretto or other
almond-flavored liqueur**
2 **tablespoons (¼ stick) unsalted
butter, room temperature**
1 **egg**
5 **peaches**
½ **cup peach or apricot preserves**

Preheat oven to 450°F. Open crust on work surface. Sprinkle with 1 tablespoon flour. Rub flour over crust, rubbing out creases. Arrange floured side down in 9-inch-diameter tart pan with removable sides. Trim and finish edges. Pierce all over with fork. Bake until light brown, about 10 minutes. Cool on rack. Reduce oven temperature to 400°F.

Finely grind slivered almonds in processor. Add remaining 1 tablespoon flour, sugar, 2 tablespoons amaretto and butter and puree. Add egg and process until well blended. Pour into crust. Bake until filling begins to brown and is springy to touch, about 15 minutes. Cool on rack. (*Can be prepared 6 hours ahead. Let stand at room temperature.*)

Bring medium pot of water to boil. Add peaches and blanch 30 seconds. Transfer to bowl of cold water, using slotted spoon. Peel peaches. Cut into slices. Drain well. Combine preserves and 1 tablespoon amaretto in heavy small saucepan. Bring to boil, stirring to melt preserves. Boil until slightly thickened, about 30 seconds. Brush some preserves over tart filling. Arrange peaches atop preserves in concentric circles, overlapping slices. Brush with remaining preserves. (*Can be prepared 3 hours ahead. Store at room temperature.*)

Fudge-Pecan Pie

*This rich southern-style pie
is great topped with scoops
of vanilla ice cream.*

8 servings

1 **cup light corn syrup**
¾ **cup sugar**
3 **ounces unsweetened chocolate,
chopped**
3 **tablespoons butter**

3 **large eggs**
1 **teaspoon vanilla extract**
¼ **teaspoon salt**
1½ **cups chopped pecans**
1 **9-inch unbaked pie crust**

Preheat oven to 350°F. Stir corn syrup and sugar in heavy medium saucepan over medium heat until sugar dissolves and mixture boils. Remove from heat. Add chocolate and butter and stir until melted and mixture is smooth. Cool slightly. Whisk in eggs, vanilla and salt. Stir in pecans. Pour filling into crust. Bake until filling is set, 40 minutes. Cool slightly. Serve warm or at room temperature.

Pear and Pine Nut Tartlets

Makes 4

Crust
- ¼ cup toasted pine nuts
- 1¼ cups unbleached all purpose flour
- ¼ cup sugar
- ¼ teaspoon salt
- 6 tablespoons (¾ stick) chilled unsalted butter, cut into ½-inch pieces
- 2 large egg yolks

Filling
- ¼ cup (½ stick) unsalted butter, room temperature
- ⅓ cup powdered sugar
- ⅛ teaspoon salt
- 2 large egg yolks
- ½ cup toasted pine nuts
- 1 tablespoon unbleached all purpose flour

- 2 small firm ripe pears, peeled, halved, cored
- 4 tablespoons pine nuts

- 2 tablespoons apricot preserves
- Mint leaves (optional)

For crust: Finely grind pine nuts with flour, sugar and salt in processor. Add butter and process until mixture resembles coarse meal. With machine running, add egg yolks and process until moist clumps form. Press together to form smooth dough. Reserve ⅓ cup (packed) dough for another use. Divide remaining dough among four 4½-inch tartlet pans with ⅝-inch-high sides and removable bottoms. Press dough firmly into bottom and up sides of each pan. Freeze until crusts are firm, about 15 minutes. (*Can be prepared up to 2 days ahead. Cover crusts and keep frozen.*)

Position rack in center of oven and preheat to 375°F. Bake crusts until pale golden, about 14 minutes. Cool. Maintain oven temperature.

For filling: Blend butter, powdered sugar and salt in processor until fluffy. Blend in yolks. Add ½ cup pine nuts and process until mixture is almost smooth, occasionally scraping down sides of work bowl. Mix in flour. Divide filling among crusts, spreading evenly.

Place pear half cut side down on work surface. Cut pear half crosswise into scant ⅛-inch-thick slices, keeping shape intact. Press pear gently to fan slices. Using small spatula as aid, transfer pear to center of tartlet atop filling. Sprinkle 1 tablespoon pine nuts over filling. Repeat with remaining pears and pine nuts.

Bake until tartlets are golden, pears are tender and filling is puffed and firm to touch, about 33 minutes. Cool.

Melt preserves in heavy small saucepan. Brush pears lightly with preserves to coat. Cool. Garnish tartlets with mint leaves if desired.

Ginger, Coconut and Papaya Tart

There's a rich cream cheese base in this simple yet sophisticated dessert.

8 servings

1 **All Ready Pie Crust (half of 15-ounce package)**
1 **tablespoon all purpose flour**

1 **8-ounce package regular or light cream cheese, room temperature**
6 **tablespoons canned cream of coconut (such as Coco Lopez)**

3 **tablespoons sugar**
1 **cup sweetened shredded coconut, lightly toasted**
¼ **cup chopped crystallized ginger**
1½ **to 2 large papayas, peeled, thinly sliced**
½ **cup apricot-pineapple preserves or apricot preserves**

Preheat oven to 450°F. Unfold crust and press out fold lines. Sprinkle with flour. Roll out to 12½-inch round. Arrange floured side down in 11-inch-diameter tart pan with removable bottom. Pierce bottom and sides with fork. Bake until golden brown, about 12 minutes. Check crust during baking; if sides of crust slide down, press up with back of fork. Cool completely.

Using electric mixer, beat cream cheese until smooth. Mix in cream of coconut and sugar, then ¾ cup coconut and ginger. Spread filling in crust. Arrange papaya attractively atop filling. Melt preserves in heavy small saucepan over low heat, stirring frequently. Brush over papaya. Sprinkle remaining ¼ cup toasted coconut around edge of tart and in center. Refrigerate until filling is firm, at least 1 hour. (*Can be prepared 6 hours ahead. Keep refrigerated.*)

Raspberry, Rhubarb and Pear Pies

Store-bought crusts make these scrumptious pies a snap to prepare.

Makes 2 pies

2 **15-ounce packages All Ready Pie Crusts**
2 **12-ounce packages frozen unsweetened raspberries, partially thawed**
1⅓ **pounds fresh rhubarb, trimmed, cut into 1-inch pieces, or 1 20-ounce package frozen rhubarb, partially thawed**
4 **cups diced peeled cored pears (about 3 medium)**

2⅓ **cups sugar**
¾ **cup plus 2 teaspoons all purpose flour**
Grated peel of 2 oranges
1 **tablespoon ground cinnamon**

1 **egg beaten with 2 tablespoons milk (glaze)**
Sugar
Vanilla ice cream or frozen yogurt

Preheat oven to 425°F. Let refrigerated pie crusts stand at room temperature 15 to 20 minutes. Combine raspberries, rhubarb, diced pears, 2⅓ cups sugar, ¾ cup all purpose flour, grated orange peel and 1 tablespoon ground cinnamon in large bowl. Mix fruit filling gently.

Unfold 2 pie crusts. Press out fold lines. Sprinkle each crust with 1 teaspoon flour; spread flour over. Place each crust floured side down in separate 10-inch-diameter pie dishes or 9-inch-diameter deep-dish pie dishes. Divide fruit filling between crusts. Press out fold lines in remaining 2 crusts. Arrange atop pies. Fold edges of top crusts under bottom crusts. Press edges together and crimp. Cut eight 1½-inch-long slits in each top crust, radiating from near center.

Brush pies with egg glaze. Sprinkle with sugar. Bake until golden brown and filling bubbles, covering edges with foil after 30 minutes, about 1 hour. Cool pies completely. Serve pies with vanilla ice cream.

Rustic Pear and Apple Tart

6 servings

Crust
1⅓ cups all purpose flour
3 tablespoons sugar
1½ teaspoons grated lemon peel
¼ teaspoon salt
¼ teaspoon ground mace
7 tablespoons cold butter, cut into ½-inch pieces
1 large egg yolk
2 tablespoons ice water

Filling
½ cup slivered almonds, toasted
2 large Golden Delicious apples, cored, cut into ½-inch-thick wedges
2 Bartlett pears, peeled, cored, cut into ½-inch-thick wedges
½ cup sugar
1½ teaspoons grated lemon peel
¼ teaspoon ground mace
1½ tablespoons butter

Whipped Cream
1 cup chilled whipping cream
2 tablespoons sugar
2 tablespoons pear schnapps or brandy

For crust: Mix flour, sugar, grated lemon peel, salt and ground mace in processor. Add butter and cut in using on/off turns until mixture resembles coarse meal. Mix yolk and water in small bowl. Add to processor and mix in using on/off turns until large moist clumps form. Gather dough into ball; flatten into disk. Wrap in waxed paper and freeze 10 minutes.

Butter 9-inch metal pie plate. Roll out dough between sheets of waxed paper to 13-inch round. Peel off top sheet of paper. Invert dough into prepared pan; peel off paper. Fold in edges to form double thickness. Crimp edges decoratively. (*Can be prepared 1 day ahead. Cover and refrigerate.*)

For filling: Preheat oven to 375°F. Finely chop slivered almonds in processor. Spread almonds on bottom of crust. Combine apples and pears in large bowl. Mix sugar, grated lemon peel and ground mace in small bowl. Toss half of sugar mixture with apples and pears. Pile into crust. Sprinkle remaining sugar mixture over fruit. Dot with 1½ tablespoons butter.

Bake until crust is brown and filling bubbles, about 1 hour. Cool on rack.

For whipped cream: Beat cream, sugar and schnapps in large bowl until medium-stiff peaks form. (*Can be prepared 4 hours ahead. Cover and chill.*)

Serve tart warm or at room temperature with whipped cream.

Puff-Pastry Pear Pie

Purchased pastry makes this impressive pie a snap.

8 servings

1 17¼-ounce package frozen puff pastry sheets (2 sheets), thawed
¼ cup plus 2 tablespoons sugar
¼ cup cornstarch
1 teaspoon vanilla extract
1 teaspoon ground cinnamon
½ teaspoon ground nutmeg
3 pounds firm but ripe pears, peeled, cored, thinly sliced
3 tablespoons butter, room temperature

Preheat oven to 400°F. Roll out 1 puff pastry sheet to 12-inch square on lightly floured surface. Line 8-inch square baking dish with 2-inch-high sides with pastry, leaving 1-inch overhang on all sides. Combine sugar and next 4 ingredients in large bowl. Add pears and toss well. Spoon pear mixture into prepared pastry. Dot top of pears with butter. Roll out second pastry sheet to 11-inch square. Brush overhang of bottom pastry with water. Top pie with second pastry sheet. Press pastry edges together to seal. Trim edges to ½ inch. Using small sharp knife, cut slits in top of pie for steam to escape. Bake until pastry is golden brown and pears are tender, about 1 hour. Serve warm or at room temperature.

Lime Tart with Berry Sauce

The lime curd that fills this tart has much less butter and fewer eggs than most.

6 servings

Filling
1½ cups sugar
¼ cup plus 1 teaspoon cornstarch
    Pinch of salt
1¼ cups water
10 tablespoons fresh lime juice
1 tablespoon plus 1 teaspoon grated lime peel
4 egg yolks, beaten to blend
2 tablespoons (¼ stick) unsalted butter

Sauce
1 16-ounce package frozen sliced strawberries with sugar, thawed
1½ tablespoons sugar
2 ½-pint baskets fresh blackberries

½ 15-ounce package All Ready Pie Crust (1 crust), room temperature
1 teaspoon all purpose flour

Very thin lime slices

For filling: Combine sugar, cornstarch and salt in heavy medium saucepan. Stir in water, lime juice and peel. Mix in yolks. Bring to boil over medium heat, stirring constantly. Boil 1 minute, stirring constantly. Remove from heat, add butter and stir until melted. Press plastic onto surface of filling and chill well.

For sauce: Combine strawberries and sugar in heavy medium saucepan. Boil until mixture is very syrupy and coats spoon thinly, stirring occasionally, about 6 minutes. Remove from heat and stir in 1 basket blackberries; cool. (*Filling and sauce can be made 1 day ahead. Cover sauce and chill both.*)

Preheat oven to 425°F. Let refrigerated crust stand at room temperature 20 minutes. Unfold crust and press out fold lines. Sprinkle with flour; spread flour over. Arrange floured side down in 9-inch-diameter tart pan with removable bottom. Fold in edges. Pierce all over with fork. Bake crust until brown, pressing up sides with back of fork if they slide down, about 12 minutes. Cool crust completely on wire rack.

Spoon filling into crust. Cover and chill until set, at least 3 hours. (*Can be prepared 6 hours ahead. Keep chilled.*)

Make 1 cut in each lime slice from center to edge; twist each slice. Alternate blackberries and lime twists around edge of tart. Cut tart into wedges, spoon berry sauce over and serve immediately.

Blueberry Streusel Tart

6 servings

Crust
1½ cups unbleached all purpose flour
3 tablespoons sugar
Pinch of salt
7 tablespoons chilled solid
   vegetable shortening
5 tablespoons chilled unsalted
   butter, cut into pieces
6 tablespoons (about) cold water

Filling
1½ cups blanched slivered almonds
¾ cup sugar
½ cup (1 stick) unsalted butter,
   room temperature

1 egg
1 tablespoon all purpose flour
1 teaspoon vanilla extract

Topping
6 tablespoons all purpose flour
6 tablespoons brown sugar
2 teaspoons ground cinnamon
2 tablespoons (¼ stick) butter

3 cups fresh blueberries or frozen,
   thawed, drained

For crust: Blend flour, sugar and salt in processor. Add shortening and butter and cut in using on/off turns until mixture resembles coarse meal. Blend in enough water by tablespoons to bind dough. Gather dough into ball; flatten into disk. Wrap in plastic and refrigerate 1 hour. (*Can be prepared 1 day ahead.*)

Preheat oven to 375°F. Roll out dough on floured surface to 13-inch round. Transfer to 11-inch-diameter tart pan with removable bottom. Press dough onto bottom and up sides of pan; trim edges. Refrigerate crust.

For filling: Finely grind almonds with sugar in processor. Add butter, egg, flour and vanilla and blend well.

For topping: Mix first 3 ingredients in small bowl. Add butter and blend with fingertips until mixture resembles coarse crumbs.

Ladle filling into crust. Top with blueberries; sprinkle topping over. Place tart on cookie sheet. Bake until crust is golden and filling is set at edges, about 1 hour. Transfer to rack and cool. Serve warm or at room temperature.

🍎 *Cakes*

Hot Fudge Banana Pound Cake

Ripples of homemade fudge sauce turn an old favorite into a deluxe treat. When topped with a scoop of vanilla ice cream and more sauce, it becomes ultra-deluxe.

10 servings

Sauce
- 1½ cups whipping cream
- 1½ cups sugar
- 6 ounces unsweetened chocolate, finely chopped
- 3 tablespoons unsalted butter
- 3 tablespoons light corn syrup
  Generous pinch of salt
- ¾ teaspoon vanilla extract

Cake
- 2 cups sifted all purpose flour
- 1 teaspoon baking powder
- ¾ teaspoon salt
- ½ teaspoon baking soda
- 1 cup (about 2 large) mashed very ripe bananas
- 1 teaspoon fresh lemon juice
- ¾ cup (1½ sticks) unsalted butter, room temperature
- 1¼ cup sugar
- 4 large eggs, room temperature

Vanilla ice cream
Fresh banana slices (optional)

For sauce: Stir whipping cream, sugar, unsweetened chocolate, unsalted butter, light corn syrup and pinch of salt in heavy medium saucepan over low heat until chocolate melts. Increase heat to medium and bring to boil, stirring occasionally. Boil until reduced to 2¾ cups, stirring constantly, about 6 minutes. Cool; mix in vanilla extract. Set aside.

For cake: Position rack in center of oven and preheat to 350°F. Lightly butter 9 × 5 × 3-inch loaf pan. Line pan with waxed paper, leaving ½-inch overhang. Sift flour, baking powder, salt and baking soda into medium bowl. Blend banana and lemon juice in small bowl. Using electric mixer, beat butter and sugar in large bowl until fluffy. Add eggs 1 at a time, beating well after each addition. Using rubber spatula, mix in dry ingredients alternately with banana mixture, beginning and ending with dry ingredients.

Heat sauce until just slightly warm, stirring often. Spoon ⅓ of batter into prepared pan. Drizzle ⅓ cup sauce over and spread gently to within ½ inch of pan edge. Repeat with another layer of batter and sauce. Top with remaining batter. Run small sharp knife through cake in zigzag motion to swirl sauce.

Bake cake until tester inserted into center comes out clean, about 1 hour 15 minutes. Cool in pan on rack 30 minutes. Turn out cake onto rack. Peel off paper and cool completely. Wrap cake in foil and store overnight at room temperature. Cover and chill remaining sauce. (*Can be prepared 2 days ahead. Let cake stand at room temperature.*)

Rewarm sauce. Cut cake crosswise into ¾-inch-thick slices. Top each with scoop of ice cream. Spoon warm sauce over. Garnish with banana slices if desired.

Chocolate Fruitcake

This is one favorite everyone will eat—guaranteed. It keeps up to three months.

16 servings

Cake

Unsweetened cocoa powder

1½ cups diced stemmed dried Calimyrna figs (about 7½ ounces)
1 cup diced pitted prunes (about 5 ounces)
1 cup diced dried peaches (about 5 ounces)
1 cup diced pitted dates (about 5 ounces)
½ cup spiced rum or dark rum
3 tablespoons minced orange peel

3 cups sifted all purpose flour
¾ cup unsweetened cocoa powder
1½ teaspoons baking powder
1½ teaspoons baking soda
¾ teaspoon ground cinnamon
¾ teaspoon salt
2 cups packed dark brown sugar
3 ounces bittersweet (not unsweetened) or semisweet chocolate, coarsely chopped

½ cup (1 stick) unsalted butter, room temperature
4 large eggs, room temperature
1 cup purchased mincemeat with brandy and rum
2½ cups (about 10 ounces) large walnut pieces, toasted

Glazes

3 tablespoons light corn syrup
2 tablespoons spiced rum or dark rum

3 ounces bittersweet (not unsweetened) or semisweet chocolate, finely chopped
3 tablespoons unsalted butter

Orange peel strips

For cake: Position rack in center of oven and preheat to 325°F. Generously butter 12-cup bundt pan. Dust pan with cocoa powder; tap out excess.

Combine next 6 ingredients. Let stand 30 minutes, stirring occasionally.

Sift flour, cocoa, baking powder, baking soda, cinnamon and salt into medium bowl. Finely grind sugar and chopped chocolate in processor.

Using electric mixer, beat butter in bowl until fluffy. Add sugar mixture in 3 additions, beating to blend after each addition (mixture will be grainy). Add eggs 1 at a time, beating well after each addition. Using rubber spatula, mix in ⅓ of dry ingredients. Mix in half of mincemeat. Mix in half of remaining dry ingredients, then remaining mincemeat. Add remaining dry ingredients and walnuts to dried fruit mixture, tossing to coat evenly. Add mixture to batter and blend thoroughly.

Spoon batter into prepared pan. Bake until tester inserted near center of cake comes out with just a few crumbs attached, covering cake loosely with foil if browning too quickly, about 1 hour 30 minutes. Let stand 20 minutes. Turn pan over onto rack. Let stand 3 minutes; gently lift off pan. Cool completely.

For glazes: Combine 3 tablespoons corn syrup and 2 tablespoons rum in bowl. Place cake on plate. Brush all of rum glaze over cake. Double-wrap in foil and store at room temperature at least 2 days. (*Can be made ahead. Store in refrigerator up to 3 months. Bring to room temperature before continuing.*)

Stir chocolate and butter in heavy small saucepan over low heat until melted and smooth. Cool approximately 15 minutes.

Drizzle chocolate glaze over top of cake in decorative pattern. Garnish with strips of orange peel and serve.

Coconut Candy Bar Cheesecake

In this rich dessert, a chewy coconut topping accents a dense chocolate filling.

12 servings

Crust

26 chocolate wafer cookies (about 6 ounces), broken into pieces
1 cup lightly packed sweetened flaked coconut
¼ cup sugar
¼ cup (½ stick) chilled unsalted butter, diced

Filling

5 ounces unsweetened chocolate, finely chopped
1 pound cream cheese, room temperature
1¾ cups sugar
3 tablespoons light corn syrup
1 teaspoon vanilla extract
1 large egg, room temperature
2 large egg yolks, room temperature

Topping

3 cups lightly packed sweetened flaked coconut (about 8 ounces)
6 tablespoons sour cream
2 ounces cream cheese, room temperature
¼ cup powdered sugar
¼ cup canned cream of coconut (such as Coco Lopez)
¼ teaspoon (scant) imitation coconut extract
⅓ cup sweetened flaked coconut, toasted

For crust: Position rack in center of oven and preheat to 350°F. Wrap outside of 9-inch springform pan with 2¾-inch-high sides with heavy-duty foil. Coarsely grind cookies, coconut and sugar in processor. Add butter and process until moist crumbs form. Press firmly onto bottom and 2 inches up sides of pan. Bake crust 10 minutes. Cool crust on rack. Maintain oven temperature.

For filling: Stir chocolate in top of double boiler over simmering water until melted and smooth. Cool.

Blend cream cheese and sugar in processor until thoroughly combined. Add melted chocolate, corn syrup and vanilla and blend, scraping down sides occasionally. Add egg and egg yolks and blend 5 seconds. Scrape down sides and blend 5 seconds. Spoon batter into crust.

Bake cheesecake until outer 2 inches are puffed and set and center is only softly set, about 40 minutes. Transfer cheesecake to wire rack; cool for 5 minutes. Maintain oven temperature.

Meanwhile, prepare topping: Blend 3 cups coconut, sour cream, cream cheese, powdered sugar, cream of coconut and extract in processor until coconut is finely chopped, scraping down sides of bowl occasionally, about 1 minute.

Gently press to flatten any raised edges of cheesecake filling. Spoon topping over and spread gently to cover filling. Bake until topping is just set and coconut just begins to brown, about 20 minutes. Transfer cheesecake to rack. Using small sharp knife, cut around cake to loosen crust from pan sides. Cool. Refrigerate cheesecake until very cold, about 4 hours. (*Can be prepared 2 days ahead. Cover and keep refrigerated.*)

Sprinkle toasted coconut over cake and serve.

Triple-Layer Devil's Food Cake

12 servings

Cake

1¾ cups water
1 tablespoon instant espresso powder or instant coffee powder
1 cup unsweetened cocoa powder

2¼ cups sifted all purpose flour
1½ teaspoons baking powder
¾ teaspoon baking soda
½ teaspoon salt
1 cup (2 sticks) unsalted butter, room temperature
2 cups firmly packed dark brown sugar (about 1 pound)
2 large eggs
2 large egg yolks

Frosting

2 vanilla beans, split lengthwise
1¼ cups whipping cream
½ cup sugar
4 large egg yolks
⅛ teaspoon salt
1 pound bittersweet (not unsweetened) or semisweet chocolate, finely chopped
¾ cup (1½ sticks) unsalted butter, cut into pieces, room temperature
½ cup light corn syrup
¼ cup sour cream

White and milk chocolate shavings

For cake: Preheat oven to 350°F. Lightly butter three 9-inch cake pans with 1¾-inch-high sides. Line pan bottoms with waxed paper rounds. Butter paper.

Bring water and coffee powder to boil in heavy small saucepan. Remove from heat. Add cocoa and whisk until smooth. Cool completely.

Sift flour, baking powder, baking soda, and salt into medium bowl. Using electric mixer, beat butter in large bowl until fluffy. Add sugar in 4 additions, beating well after each addition and scraping down sides of bowl occasionally. Add eggs and yolks 1 at a time, beating just to blend after each addition. Using rubber spatula, mix dry ingredients into butter mixture alternately with cocoa mixture, beginning and ending with dry ingredients. Divide batter evenly among prepared pans. Bake until toothpick inserted into centers comes out clean, about 23 minutes. Cool cakes in pans on racks 10 minutes. Turn out onto racks. Peel off waxed paper; cool completely. (*Can be prepared 1 day ahead. Return cakes to pans and cover tightly with foil. Let stand at room temperature.*)

For frosting: Carefully scrape seeds from vanilla beans into heavy large saucepan (save beans for another use). Add cream, sugar, yolks and salt and blend well. Stir over medium-low heat until custard thickens and leaves path on back of spoon when finger is drawn across, about 7 minutes; do not boil. Mix in chocolate, butter and corn syrup. Remove from heat; stir until smooth. Mix in sour cream. Transfer frosting to bowl and refrigerate until spreadable, stirring occasionally, approximately 1 hour.

Place 1 cake layer on platter. Spread 1 cup frosting over. Repeat with second cake layer and frosting. Top with third cake layer. Spread remaining frosting over top and sides of cake, swirling decoratively. (*Can be made 1 day ahead. Cover with cake dome and chill. Let stand at room temperature 1 hour.*)

Sprinkle white and milk chocolate shavings thickly over top of cake.

Poppy Seed Cake with Orange Glaze

8 servings

Cake
2¾ cups sugar
1 cup corn oil
3 large eggs
1½ teaspoons vanilla extract
1 teaspoon almond extract
3 cups all purpose flour
2 tablespoons poppy seeds

1½ teaspoons baking powder
½ teaspoon salt
1½ cups milk

Glaze
1 cup powdered sugar
¼ cup orange juice
¼ teaspoon almond extract

For cake: Preheat oven to 350°F. Grease and flour 12-cup bundt pan. Using electric mixer, beat first 5 ingredients in large bowl to blend. Mix flour, poppy seeds, baking powder and salt in medium bowl. Stir dry ingredients alternately with milk into sugar mixture, beginning and ending with dry ingredients. Pour batter into prepared pan. Bake until tester inserted near center comes out clean, about 50 minutes. Cool cake in pan on rack 10 minutes.

Meanwhile, prepare glaze: Whisk all ingredients in small bowl to blend. Turn out cake onto rack. Spoon glaze over warm cake. Cool completely.

Banana Upside-Down Cake

Serves 6

1 cup firmly packed light brown sugar
6 tablespoons (¾ stick) unsalted butter, room temperature
2 large ripe bananas, sliced

1½ cups cake flour
¾ teaspoon baking soda
½ teaspoon baking powder

½ teaspoon salt
1 cup mashed ripe bananas (about 2)
½ cup buttermilk
1 teaspoon vanilla extract
1¼ cups sugar
⅓ cup vegetable shortening
2 eggs

Position rack in lowest third of oven and preheat to 350°F. Using electric mixer, cream brown sugar and butter in medium bowl until well mixed. Spread brown sugar mixture over bottom of 9-inch square baking dish with 2-inch-high sides. Arrange banana slices atop brown sugar mixture, covering completely.

Combine flour, baking soda, baking powder and salt in small bowl. Mix mashed bananas, buttermilk and vanilla in another small bowl. Using electric mixer, cream 1¼ cups sugar and shortening until fluffy. Add eggs 1 at a time, beating well after each addition. Add dry ingredients alternately with buttermilk mixture, mixing until just combined. Pour batter over bananas in pan. Bake until cake pulls away from sides of pan and tester inserted into center of cake comes out clean, about 1 hour 5 minutes. Transfer to rack and cool slightly. Turn cake out onto plate. Serve warm or at room temperature.

Sunshine Cheesecake

This treat is topped with slices of bright oranges. The slices must be cooked very slowly, or the pulp will fall away. Begin preparing the cheesecake one day before you plan to serve it.

10 to 12 servings

Crust
1½ 8-ounce bags gingersnap cookies, ground (about 3 cups)
6 tablespoons (¾ stick) butter, melted
1½ teaspoons (generous) minced orange peel (orange part only)

Filling
1½ cups orange juice
1 3-inch piece unpeeled fresh ginger, thinly sliced (about ⅓ cup)
4 8-ounce packages cream cheese, room temperature

⅔ cup sugar
1 tablespoon minced orange peel (orange part only)
1 tablespoon vanilla extract
8 ounces imported white chocolate (such as Lindt), melted
4 large eggs

Candied Oranges
4 cups water
2 cups sugar
3 seedless oranges (unpeeled), cut into paper-thin slices

Fresh mint leaves

For crust: Stir all ingredients in medium bowl until crumbs are moist. Press crumbs onto bottom and 2 inches up sides of 9 × 2¾-inch springform pan.

For filling: Preheat oven to 350°F. Boil orange juice and ginger in heavy medium saucepan until reduced to 3 tablespoons, about 12 minutes. Using electric mixer, beat cream cheese, sugar, orange peel and vanilla in large bowl until smooth. Strain reduced orange juice and add to bowl. With mixer running, add chocolate and beat until combined. Reduce speed to low. Add eggs 1 at a time, beating until just combined.

Pour batter into crust. Bake cheesecake until top is dry and sides puff slightly (most of cheesecake will jiggle when shaken), about 50 minutes. Transfer to rack and cool. Cover and chill overnight. (*Can be prepared 2 days ahead.*)

For oranges: Cover rack with waxed paper. Combine water and sugar in heavy wide shallow pot. Stir over medium heat until sugar dissolves. Simmer 5 minutes. Add orange slices 1 at a time. Adjust heat so syrup bubbles only around edges of pan. Cook oranges 1 hour. Turn over top layer of oranges and cook until oranges are translucent and orange peels are tender, about 1 hour longer. Arrange oranges in single layer on prepared rack. Let dry 1 hour. Boil sugar syrup until thick, about 6 minutes. (*Can be prepared 6 hours ahead.*)

Run small knife around edges of cheesecake. Loosen pan sides and remove. Overlap orange slices atop cheesecake. Reheat orange syrup over low heat if necessary. Brush over orange slices. Garnish with mint and serve.

French Apple Cake

8 servings

¼ cup (½ stick) unsalted butter
1¾ cups sugar
⅓ cup water
¾ teaspoon ground cinnamon
2 large Granny Smith apples (about 1¼ pounds), peeled, cored, thinly sliced

1 cup all purpose flour
1 teaspoon baking powder

¼ teaspoon salt
3 large egg yolks
2 large eggs
2 tablespoons Calvados, applejack or other brandy
2 teaspoons vanilla
½ cup (1 stick) unsalted butter, melted

Preheat oven to 350°F. Butter 9-inch-diameter cake pan with 2-inch-high sides. Coat pan with sugar; tap out excess. Melt ¼ cup butter in heavy large skillet over medium-high heat. Stir in ¾ cup sugar, water and cinnamon and bring to boil. Add apples and cook until apples are just tender, turning frequently, about 15 minutes. Remove apples, using slotted spoon, and arrange decoratively in bottom of pan. Continue boiling liquid in skillet until thick and syrupy, about 4 minutes. Pour over apples.

Sift flour, baking powder and salt into small bowl. Whisk remaining 1 cup sugar, egg yolks, eggs, Calvados and vanilla in large bowl to blend. Gently stir in dry ingredients. Fold in ½ cup melted butter. Pour batter over apples in pan. Bake until toothpick inserted into center of cake comes out clean, about 45 minutes. Cool cake in pan 5 minutes. Run small sharp knife around side of pan to loosen cake. Turn cake out onto platter. Serve warm or at room temperature.

Double-Ginger Gingerbread with Orange-Ginger Sauce

This homespun dessert gets a modern twist: It's filled with chopped crystallized ginger and topped with an orange-ginger sauce.

8 servings

1½ cups all purpose flour
1 teaspoon baking soda
1 teaspoon ground ginger
1 teaspoon ground cinnamon
½ teaspoon salt
½ teaspoon pepper
½ cup (1 stick) unsalted butter, room temperature
½ cup packed dark brown sugar

2 eggs
¼ cup dark molasses
⅔ cup buttermilk
¼ cup chopped crystallized ginger

½ cup chilled whipping cream, whipped to soft peaks
Orange-Ginger Sauce (see recipe)

Preheat oven to 325°F. Butter 8-inch square cake pan; dust with flour. Sift first 6 ingredients into small bowl. Using electric mixer, beat butter in large bowl until light and fluffy. Add sugar and beat until fluffy. Add eggs 1 at a time, beating well after each addition. Mix in molasses. Mix in half of dry ingredients, then buttermilk, then remaining dry ingredients. Fold in crystallized ginger.

Transfer batter to prepared pan. Bake until tester inserted into center of cake comes out clean, about 45 minutes. Cool cake slightly in pan on rack. (*Can be made 6 hours ahead. Cool. Cover with foil and rewarm 10 minutes at 375°F.*)

Cut warm cake into squares and place on plates. Top with cream and Orange-Ginger Sauce and serve.

Orange-Ginger Sauce

*Also delicious over scoops
of vanilla ice cream or
frozen yogurt.*

Makes about 1½ cups

3 large oranges
1 cup (about) orange juice
6 tablespoons sugar

1 cinnamon stick
3 tablespoons chopped crystallized
ginger

Cut peel and white pith from oranges. Working over small bowl, cut between membranes of oranges with small sharp knife, releasing segments. Transfer segments to medium bowl. Pour accumulated orange juice into measuring cup. Add enough orange juice to measure 1 cup plus 2 tablespoons. Transfer juice to medium saucepan. Add sugar and cinnamon. Cook over low heat, stirring until sugar dissolves. Increase heat and simmer until juice mixture is syrupy and reduced to 6 tablespoons, about 12 minutes. Pour over oranges. Add ginger. Cool. (*Sauce can be made 1 day ahead. Cover and refrigerate.*)

Chocolate, Plum and Walnut Torte

8 servings

Cake
8 ounces semisweet chocolate,
  chopped
½ cup (1 stick) unsalted butter, cut
  into 8 pieces, room temperature
⅔ cup sugar
3 eggs
½ cup cake flour
¾ cup chopped walnuts
  (about 3 ounces)

Glaze
3 tablespoons whipping cream
3 tablespoons slivovitz or other
  brandy
1 tablespoon light corn syrup
5½ ounces semisweet chocolate,
  chopped
⅓ cup plum jam or apricot
  preserves
½ cup chopped walnuts

For cake: Preheat oven to 350°F. Butter 8-inch-diameter cake pan with 2-inch-high sides. Line bottom with parchment; butter paper. Dust pan with flour. Melt chocolate in top of double boiler over simmering water. Remove from over water. Add butter 1 piece at a time, mixing until melted and smooth. Mix in sugar. Mix in eggs 1 at a time. Add flour, then walnuts and stir to combine. Transfer batter to prepared cake pan. Bake just until springy to touch, about 45 minutes. Cool cake in pan on rack 15 minutes. Turn out onto rack, remove parchment paper and cool completely.

For glaze: Bring whipping cream, slivovitz and light corn syrup to simmer in heavy medium saucepan. Reduce heat to low. Add semisweet chocolate and whisk until melted and smooth. Let glaze stand until cool but still pourable, whisking occasionally.

Place cake on serving platter. Slide waxed paper under edges. Spread jam over top. Pour glaze over top and sides of cake. Smooth top and sides with spatula. Sprinkle walnuts in 1-inch border around top edge. Let stand until glaze sets. (*Torte can be prepared 1 day ahead. Cover tightly and refrigerate. Bring to room temperature before serving.*)

Fudge Cake with Ice Cream and Caramel Sauce

12 servings

Sauce
1 cup sugar
6 tablespoons water
2 teaspoons cream of tartar
½ cup plus 2 tablespoons whipping cream
¼ cup (½ stick) unsalted butter

Cake
¾ cup unsweetened cocoa powder
1 cup plus 2 tablespoons boiling water

¾ cup (1½ sticks) unsalted butter, room temperature
2¼ cups sugar
3 large eggs
1½ teaspoons vanilla extract
2¼ cups all purpose flour
1½ teaspoons baking soda
¾ teaspoon salt
1½ cups sour cream

Vanilla ice cream

For sauce: Cook sugar, water and cream of tartar in heavy medium saucepan over medium-low heat, stirring until sugar dissolves. Increase heat to medium-high and cook without stirring until syrup turns deep golden brown, swirling pan occasionally. Remove from heat. Gradually add cream (mixture will bubble vigorously) and stir until smooth. Add butter and whisk until melted. (*Can be made 1 day ahead. Cover and refrigerate. Before serving, rewarm over low heat.*)

For cake: Preheat oven to 350°F. Grease 9 × 13-inch baking pan. Place cocoa in metal bowl. Gradually add boiling water, stirring constantly. Cool.

Using electric mixer, cream butter with sugar in large bowl. Add eggs 1 at a time, beating well after each addition. Beat in vanilla. Mix flour, baking soda and salt in bowl. Stir into butter mixture alternately with sour cream. Stir in cocoa mixture. Pour batter into prepared pan. Bake until toothpick inserted into center of cake comes out clean, about 50 minutes. Cool cake slightly on rack.

Cut warm cake into squares. Divide among plates. Top with scoop of ice cream. Pour caramel sauce over.

❦ Cookies

Cornmeal Guava Thumbprint Cookies

Serve these easy-to-make cookies with a toss of tropical fruits, such as mango, pineapple, papaya and banana.

Makes about 2 dozen

1 cup all purpose flour
⅓ cup cornmeal
½ teaspoon ground cinnamon
½ teaspoon ground nutmeg
⅛ teaspoon salt
½ cup (1 stick) unsalted butter, room temperature

½ cup firmly packed brown sugar
1 egg yolk
¾ teaspoon vanilla extract

Guava jelly or apricot-pineapple preserves

Preheat oven to 350°F. Combine flour, cornmeal, ground cinnamon, nutmeg and salt in medium bowl. Using electric mixer, beat butter and brown sugar in large bowl until fluffy. Mix in egg yolk and vanilla. Mix in dry ingredients.

Form dough into 1-inch balls. Arrange on ungreased baking sheet, spacing 1½ inches apart. Make depression in center of each using thumb or handle of wooden spoon. Bake 10 minutes. Fill depressions with jelly. Continue baking until bottoms of cookies are brown, about 10 minutes. Cool on rack. (*Can be prepared 1 week ahead. Refrigerate in airtight container.*)

Lemon Hazelnut Squares

Makes 16

Crust
1 cup all purpose flour
¼ cup sugar
¼ teaspoon salt
6 tablespoons (¾ stick) chilled unsalted butter, cut into pieces
¼ cup chopped husked toasted hazelnuts

Filling
¾ cup sugar
2 eggs
3 tablespoons fresh lemon juice
1 tablespoon minced lemon zest
½ teaspoon baking powder
Pinch of salt

Powdered sugar

For crust: Preheat oven to 350°F. Line 8-inch square baking pan with foil; butter foil. Mix flour, sugar and salt in processor. Add butter and nuts and blend until fine meal forms. Press onto bottom of prepared pan. Bake until light brown around edges, about 18 minutes.

Meanwhile, prepare filling: Blend first 6 ingredients in processor.

Pour filling onto hot crust. Bake until filling begins to brown at edges and is just springy to touch, about 20 minutes. Cool completely in pan on rack.

Lift foil and dessert from pan. Gently peel foil from edges. Cut dessert into 16 squares. (*Can be made 1 day ahead. Wrap tightly; chill.*) Sift powdered sugar over squares; serve at room temperature.

Spiced Molasses Ginger Cookies

These cookies are crunchy outside, soft and chewy inside. They're terrific with a glass of milk or a cup of tea, and kids love them in their lunch boxes.

Makes about 36

2 cups sifted all purpose flour
2 teaspoons baking soda
2 teaspoons ground cinnamon
1½ teaspoons ground ginger
1 teaspoon ground cloves
1 teaspoon salt
½ cup solid vegetable shortening

¼ cup (½ stick) unsalted butter, room temperature
1 cup firmly packed golden brown sugar
1 egg
¼ cup dark molasses

Ice water
Sugar

Preheat oven to 350°F. Lightly butter cookie sheets. Sift first 6 ingredients into medium bowl. Using electric mixer, beat shortening, butter and brown sugar in large bowl until fluffy. Add egg and molasses to butter mixture and beat until blended. Mix in dry ingredients. Refrigerate dough 1 hour.

Roll dough into 1¼-inch balls. Dip quickly into ice water, then roll in sugar to coat. Arrange on prepared cookie sheets, spacing 2 inches apart. Bake until cookies are pale golden and cracked on top but still soft to touch, about 10 minutes. Let stand 1 minute. Using metal spatula, transfer to rack and cool completely. Store cookies in airtight container.

Chocolate Chunk Cookies

Makes about 40

2½ cups old-fashioned oats
2 cups all purpose flour
1 teaspoon baking powder
1 teaspoon baking soda
½ teaspoon salt
1 cup (2 sticks) unsalted butter, room temperature
1 cup sugar

1 cup firmly packed golden brown sugar
2 eggs
1 teaspoon vanilla extract
12 ounces semisweet chocolate, cut into ½-inch chunks
1½ cups chopped pecans (about 6 ounces)
4 ounces milk chocolate, grated

Preheat oven to 350°F. Butter cookie sheets. Finely grind oats in processor. Transfer to large bowl. Add flour, baking powder, baking soda and salt to oats and blend well. Using electric mixer, beat butter and both sugars in another large bowl until light and fluffy. Beat in eggs and vanilla. Mix in dry ingredients. Fold in semisweet chocolate, pecans and milk chocolate.

Form dough into 1¼-inch balls. Arrange dough on prepared cookie sheets, spacing 2 inches apart. Bake until cookies are pale golden, about 10 minutes. Transfer cookies to rack and cool completely. Store airtight.

Lemon Pudding Cookies

Makes about 20

1 cup buttermilk baking mix
1 3.4-ounce package instant lemon
   pudding

1 large egg, beaten to blend
¼ cup vegetable oil
   Sugar

Preheat oven to 350°F. Grease 2 large cookie sheets. Mix first 4 ingredients in large bowl until dough forms. Roll dough into 1-inch balls. Place balls 2 inches apart on prepared cookie sheets. Dip flat-bottom glass into sugar. Press glass onto dough ball and flatten into ¼-inch-thick cookie. Repeat with remaining cookies. Bake until just golden brown on edges, about 10 minutes. Transfer to racks and cool completely. (*Can be prepared 3 days ahead. Store airtight.*)

White Chocolate Chunk Brownies

12 servings

3 tablespoons instant coffee powder
1 tablespoon water
2 cups firmly packed brown sugar
¾ cup (1½ sticks) unsalted butter
2 large eggs
2 tablespoons coffee liqueur
2 cups all purpose flour

2 teaspoons baking powder
½ teaspoon salt
5 ounces white chocolate, cut into
   ¾-inch pieces
¾ cup coarsely chopped pecans,
   toasted

Preheat oven to 350°F. Butter 10-inch-diameter cake pan. Line bottom with parchment. Combine coffee powder and 1 tablespoon water in heavy medium saucepan. Stir over medium-low heat until coffee dissolves. Add sugar and butter and stir until butter melts. Pour into large bowl and cool to room temperature, stirring occasionally. Add eggs and coffee liqueur to butter mixture and whisk to combine. Sift flour, baking powder and salt into small bowl. Add to butter mixture and stir to blend. Stir in chocolate and pecans.

Pour batter into prepared pan. Bake until tester inserted into center comes out almost clean, about 35 minutes. Cool in pan on rack. Run small sharp knife around sides of pan to loosen brownie. Turn out onto plate; peel off parchment. Cut into wedges and serve.

Oatmeal, Date, Pecan and Chocolate Chip Cookies

Just the thing for a late-night snack. Try a couple with a glass of ice-cold milk and a movie on the VCR.

Makes about 2 dozen

1½ cups old-fashioned oatmeal
½ cup all purpose flour
1 teaspoon baking soda
1 teaspoon baking powder
½ cup (1 stick) unsalted butter, room temperature
⅔ cup firmly packed dark brown sugar
½ cup sugar

1 egg
1 teaspoon vanilla extract
¾ cup chopped pitted dates (about 5 ounces)
¾ cup chopped pecans (about 3 ounces)
⅔ cup semisweet chocolate chips

Preheat oven to 375°F. Grease 2 heavy large cookie sheets. Mix first 4 ingredients together in medium bowl. Using electric mixer, cream butter and both sugars in large bowl until light and fluffy. Beat in egg and vanilla. Mix in oatmeal mixture. Stir in remaining ingredients. Drop rounded tablespoons of dough about 2 inches apart onto prepared cookie sheets. Flatten cookies slightly with spoon. Bake until brown, about 10 minutes. Cool 5 minutes on cookie sheets. Transfer cookies to rack and cool completely. (*Can be prepared 4 days ahead. Store in airtight container.*)

Rocky Road Wedges

Makes 24 wedges

1 cup (2 sticks) unsalted butter, room temperature
1 cup firmly packed brown sugar
2 eggs
1¾ cups all purpose flour
¼ cup unsweetened cocoa powder
1 teaspoon baking soda
½ teaspoon salt

3 cups semisweet chocolate chips (about 18 ounces)
1 cup whole almonds, coarsely choppped (about 6 ounces)

1 cup mini marshmallows

Rocky road ice cream

Preheat oven to 350°F. Cream butter and sugar in large bowl until fluffy. Beat in eggs. Combine flour, cocoa powder, baking soda and salt in bowl. Stir dry ingredients into butter mixture. Mix in 2 cups chocolate chips and almonds.

Divide dough in half. On back of ungreased baking sheet, pat each half into 8-inch round. Bake until cookies are set but centers are still soft, about 15 minutes. Sprinkle each round with ½ cup mini marshmallows and ½ cup chocolate chips. Bake until marshmallows and chips soften, about 3 minutes longer. Cool 5 minutes. Cut each round into 12 wedges. Slide wedges off baking sheet and cool completely on rack.

Top wedges with rocky road ice cream.

Index

News '92

The Year of Food and Entertaining in Review

Trends and New Products

Foods and Info by Mail

Books

Restaurants and People

Getaways

For the Kitchen and Table

Diet News

❦ *Trends and New Products*

CAUSE A STIR

Swizzle sticks are back in fashion, and Murano makes some beautiful glass ones. The 6-inch jewel-tone designs are available in several styles and colors for $8 each, plus shipping, from the Frank McIntosh boutique at Henri Bendel in New York. To order, telephone 212-373-6367.

❦

COOL KEEPER

Tired of lugging that big old ice chest around? Thermalwhiz Lifestyle Coolers are lightweight, leakproof, easy to clean and fold down flat for storage. They're available in two sizes: 6-quart capacity for about $15, and a 24-quart version for $20. For store locations, telephone 416-590-7700.

❦

BURN THIS

Because it's from the slow-growing hardwood forests of northern Quebec, Nature's Own aged maple chunk charwood burns hotter and longer than ordinary charcoal. The maple is harvested in accordance with such forest-saving techniques as selective tree cutting, and it's fired in reduced-pollution kilns. An 8.8-pound bag costs about $7 to $10 in selected retail stores. For locations, telephone 800-BUY-CHAR or 508-226-4710.

❦

ECO GLASS

The "Confetti" glassware from Mesa International is made of recycled glass, so you'll be environmentally correct with every sip. It is available in two color combinations, including the cheerful orange, yellow, green and blue "Mardi Gras" pattern. The 2½-quart pitcher is about $30; an 18-ounce tumbler is approximately $8. Call 603-526-2127 for locations.

❦

PICTURE THIS

Los Angeles designer Stephanie Blank uses a variety of antique food and drink labels to produce her original handmade picture frames. An 8x10-inch frame is $76, plus shipping (smaller sizes are also available). Call 310-828-2801 to order.

LETTUCE SAY THANKS

Collectible Greetings has taken old-fashioned lithographed seed packets and turned them into cards that are just the right size for a quick thank-you note or dinner invitation. Ten assorted vegetable cards with envelopes are $28; a pack of four assorted herb cards with envelopes is $13. To order, telephone 508-443-8471.

IT'S IN THE BAG

For an impromptu picnic or quick trip to the market, be sure to pack along the Shopping Bag in a Wallet. It folds down to 6½ by 3 inches (keep it in your purse or pocket). Made of washable polyethylene mesh and nylon with Velcro closures, it costs $12 plus shipping. Call 310-459-1719 to order.

RACK 'EM UP

Peter R. Root, a California architect turned artist, calls his one-of-a-kind pot racks three-dimensional paintings. The one titled "Eat," which spells out the word and comes adorned with lemons, a steer's head and sausages, among other things, is made of wood and steel and is about 30 inches wide and 18 inches tall. The price is $350 plus shipping; other pieces range from $300 up to $900 for larger, custom-designed works. Call 310-458-8013 for details.

❦

GARDEN FRESH

The fresh herb basket from Malibu Greens ($25) is a terrific gift for your favorite cook. Also available are baskets of baby lettuces ($25), baby vegetables ($38), and a combination of exotic fruits and baby vegetables ($55). Call 800-383-1414 to order.

HOT PANTS

Even if you aren't a chef, you'll look like a pro in the all-cotton chef's pants from Chefwear. They're $33, plus shipping, and come in solid black or white or a black-and-white or red-and-white houndstooth check in unisex sizes, from extra small to double extra large. To order, telephone 800-568-CHEF.

GREAT DANE

Aquavit, a traditional distilled spirit from Denmark, is making quite a splash stateside in a new incarnation, Jubilaeum. A flavored vodka with hints of herbs and citrus, it's delicious right out of the freezer, mixed with club soda or served on the rocks. (And you should taste what it does to a Bloody Mary.) The eye-catching, three-sided bottle costs about $22.95; for store locations or mail-order, call 708-948-8888, ext. 517.

FRUITY MIXERS

Intensely flavored but not too sweet, the sodas from Mad River Traders are a grown-up's answer to soft drinks. Available in ten flavors (cranberry sea breeze is our favorite), they're also terrific mixers. A 12-ounce bottle costs about 95 cents at Macy's and specialty foods stores. Call 802-253-4535 for a location near you.

FRUIT DROPS

Fellow food lovers are sure to be dazzled by the charming earrings designed by California pastry chef Lynette Cline. The glass grapes, pears, apples, eggplant, carrots and bell peppers on sterling wire cost $35 per pair. Order by calling 415-982-6518.

VEGGIE TIMES

Mark the time with porcelain tomatoes, radishes, corn and other veggies on a ceramic plate wall clock from Wireless. The 10¼-inch-diameter clock will set you back only $50, plus shipping (and, of course, one AA battery). Call 800-669-9999 and specify no. 20003.

🌺 *Foods and Info by Mail*

MIDWEST CHESHIRE

Loomis Cheese Company of Ann Arbor, Michigan, has introduced the superbly balanced Great Lakes Cheshire Cheese. Nutty, tangy and buttery, it's available at select specialty foods stores and cheese shops for about $8 a pound. Or for mail order call Zingerman's at 313-663-3400.

FABULOUS FINALE

Want a triple chocolate treat? The Chocolate Macadamia Nut Pie from Finalés Gourmet Desserts has a chocolate shortbread crust that's layered with chocolate chips and macadamia nuts and topped with a chocolate filigree. A 10-inch-diameter pie is $19.95, plus shipping. Telephone 800-926-8194 or 206-778-8094 to order.

BREAD AND SPREAD

Here's a winning combo from Massachusetts: sweet and tart cider jelly from Greenwood Farms and stone-ground sourdough breads from Berkshire Mountain Bakery. Each loaf (there's a variety of flavors, from whole wheat to rye sesame) is about $2.50, plus shipping. Order by calling Bread & Stuff at 413-274-6346. For the jelly (a pack of three 9-ounce jars is $12.75, plus shipping), call 413-498-5995.

WHAT A TREAT

Made with the richest caramel and milk chocolate and the best nuts, Fran's Park Bar with Peanuts makes a rewarding afternoon snack. A gift box of eight 1¾-ounce bars is $14, plus shipping. Call 206-322-6511 to order.

UP FROM DOWN UNDER

Anzac cookies, cherished treats for generations of Australian and New Zealand children, are making a big splash stateside. Now made in the U.S.A., they're available half-dipped in white and milk chocolate in 24-ounce pails for $25 and 12-ounce gift boxes for $9. To order, call Down Under Delights, 415-365-8258 or 800-24-KOALA.

MAIL-ORDER LAMB

For years Jamison Farm in western Pennsylvania has been providing some of the country's finest restaurants with additive-free, naturally raised lamb. Now you can get some for your next dinner party: Tender rib and loin chops are delivered to your door for $110 (twenty-four 4-ounce chops), plus shipping. To order or to get details on other cuts (and their lamb sauce for pasta), call 800-237-LAMB.

HOT STUFF

The jam-packed Southwest Basket from Frieda's Inc. makes a terrific gift for those who love spicy cuisine. The goodies include an array of dried chilies, chayote squash, plantain bananas, jicama and spicy rice, plus all the fixin's for making tamales (and much more). The price is $62; to order, phone 800-241-1771 or 213-627-2981.

HERE'S THE BEEF

If you appreciate quality beef, you'll want to order Tenderloin Ka-Bobs from Omaha Steaks International. They arrive ready to grill or broil, with each skewer holding a combination of aged beef, bell peppers and mushrooms. Six 8-ounce Ka-Bobs are $46, plus shipping; 12 of the Ka-Bobs are $77. Call 800-228-9055 to order.

WHAT A PAIR

Larry Forgione's Barbecue Mustard from American Spoon Foods and Goldwater's Bisbee Barbeque Ketchup (with the smoky flavor of *chipotle* chilies) take burgers and hot dogs to new gastronomic heights. An 8-ounce jar of the very spicy mustard is $4.25, plus shipping; call 800-222-5886 or 616-347-9030. For the catsup (one 14-ounce jar is about $3 to $5), order from Dean & DeLuca, 800-221-7714, or A.J.'s, 800-578-5037.

RELISH TO RELISH

Vidalia onions star in the Old Port Republic sweet relish from Sea Island Mercantile & Provisioning. Three 8½-ounce jars cost $14.50. To order, call 800-735-3215 or 803-522-3000.

GET YOUR GOAT

The aged New York State goat cheese with green peppercorns from Coach Dairy Goat Farm has a wonderful, distinctive flavor—mellow and sharp at the same time. It's $16 a pound, plus shipping, from Zingerman's in Ann Arbor, Michigan; 313-663-3400.

ALMONDS JOY

Larguetta almonds have a bit sweeter taste and a longer, more cylindrical shape than their American cousins. Grown only in the Reus district of northeast Spain, they're available stateside in a 1½-pound tin for $22.95, plus shipping, from The Squire's Choice catalog; telephone 800-523-6163.

WINNING BASKET

Balducci's has made it easy to cook up a delicious paella feast. Their elaborate gift basket comes overflowing with all the essentials—Spanish olive oil, rice, saffron, chorizo sausages, smoked mussels—even a clay paella casserole pan (and that's just the start of it). It's $140, plus shipping. To order, telephone 800-225-3822.

WHAT A JAM

The olallieberry—a cross between a black loganberry and a youngberry—is a tart-sweet fruit that makes a delectable jam. It's particularly good on warm scones or biscuits. An 8-ounce jar from Morin's Landing is $4.95, plus shipping; gift packs are also available. Call 800-547-1511.

SAY CHEESE

Elegantly wrapped in chestnut leaves, the sheep's milk cheese from Washington State is a flavorful, nutty, semisoft farmhouse cheese. It's available from Balducci's for $26 a pound (shipping costs extra); call 800-225-3822.

FUNGI FETTISH

Attention, fungi lovers: We've uncovered a good mail-order company for fresh *shiitake* mushrooms. It's Delftree Farm in the Berkshire Mountains of Massachusetts. Firm and meaty, the shiitakes are shipped in a linen storage bag in 2-pound boxes, with recipes included, for about $32 and arrive the next day. Call 800-243-3742.

DUTCH TREAT

The Pennsylvania Dutch are famous for shoofly pie, a rich, old-fashioned dessert with a dark, moist filling and spicy crumb topping. Miller's Smorgasbord Bakery makes one of the best, and it's only $9.95, including shipping ($3 higher, though, if you live west of the Mississippi). To order yours, telephone 800-669-3568.

SWEET THINGS

Rich, flaky *rugelach* are just the right size for when you want a taste of something sweet. Made by Chewys in San Diego, the pastries are filled with a variety of fruits, nuts and spices. A forty-piece assorted gift package costs $40 (shipping included). To order, telephone 800-241-3456.

PEACE OF CHOCOLATE

Not only are these bars the stuff chocolate fantasies are made of, but eating them could also help make the world a better place. Cloud Nine contributes 10 percent of its profits to the conservation of rain forests and an additional 1 percent of profits to the "1% for Peace" organization. The nine flavors range from malted milk crunch to sun-dried cherry; each 3¼-ounce bar costs about $1.89. Call 201-216-0382 to place your order.

BOUQUET IN A BOTTLE

What cook wouldn't want a stunning bottle of herb vinegar on the cupboard shelf? Better yet—how about a little in a sauce or salad? Flavored with organically grown herbs and edible flowers, the vinegar from Fredericksburg Herb Farm is mildly tangy with a hint of fennel and spice. A 25.4-ounce bottle is $20 plus shipping. To order, telephone 800-284-0526.

THAT'S AMORE

Treat your sweetie to a box of Italian confections from Perugina's "Romantic Nights Collection." Packaged in pretty heart-shaped boxes with blue starry backgrounds, the samplers range from assorted chocolates to chocolate cherries to Baci, Perugina's luscious dark chocolate and hazelnut "kisses." Prices start at $13.50. Available at major department stores, or call 800-272-0500 or, in New York City, 800-688-2490 to order.

APPLE OF OUR EYE

To make their chunky applesauce, Hawkins Homemade takes only tart Pippin apples and adds a touch of honey, lemon and cinnamon. Spoon it on top of ice cream or spread it on hot biscuits—it's delicious any which way. About $5.75 per 12¼-ounce jar, the sauce is available through the Seyco Fine Food catalog; 800-423-2942.

RECYCLING DEMYSTIFIED

"Sensible Consumption, a Guide to Conservation in the Kitchen" is a straightforward, easy-to-understand, free booklet that demystifies recycling terminology. It's a must for the modern kitchen. To order, write California Table Grape Commission, P.O. Box 5498, Fresno, CA 93755.

MONDO SWEETS

The Mondel Bread from the Anna, Ida & Me bakery in Chicago is nutty, crunchy and has just the right touch of sweetness. It's available in ten delicious flavors from raspberry ribbon to peanut butter crunch. Look for 3- and 8-ounce packages in specialty foods stores, or for a wide selection of mail-order items, call 800-729-ANNA.

CALIFORNIA NUTS

Pistachio fans will love the butter-toffee-coated nuts from Pacific Gold. And if that doesn't sound scrumptious enough, how about pistachios dipped in dark chocolate? A set of three large bags—butter-toffee, dark chocolate and salted—in a wooden crate is available from specialty foods stores for about $22.50. Call 209-661-6176 for additional information.

🍎 *Books*

SOUTHERN TWANG

Beth Tartan's new revised edition of *North Carolina & Old Salem Cookery* (University of North Carolina Press, 1992) is a delightful collection of regional history, reminiscences and recipes. And in *How to Eat Like a Southerner and Live to Tell the Tale* (Clarkson Potter, 1992), Courtney Parker lightens up traditional southern dishes, deliciously.

🍎

HELPING THE HUNGRY . . .

. . . That's the idea behind *Five Star Recipes for Healthy Eating* (U.S. Healthcare, 1992), a book of healthful recipes from twenty-one top chefs and restaurants across the country. It's produced jointly by Share Our Strength (S.O.S.), a network of food industry professionals united to fight hunger, and U.S. Healthcare, a leading operator of health-maintenance organizations. Proceeds from the book benefit hunger-relief groups. For a copy, mail a check for $12.95 payable to S.O.S. to *Five Star Recipes for Healthy Eating* Cookbook, c/o S.O.S. National Office, 1511 K Street, NW, Suite 940, Washington, DC 20005.

🍎

ETHNIC GOES LIGHT

A couple of new books are just the thing for cooks looking for easy, low-calorie ethnic recipes. *Italian Light Cooking* and *Mexican Light Cooking* (Perigee Books, 1992) by Marie Simmons and Kathi Long, respectively, present new takes on traditional recipes. Included are recipes for everything from pizza to pesto and nachos to tacos. All are low in calories, with reduced fat and cholesterol.

A SPLENDID READ

In her new book, *The Splendid Table,* subtitled *500 Years of Eating in Northern Italy* (William Morrow, 1992), Lynne Rossetto Kasper presents over two hundred traditional recipes from the famed Emilia-Romagna region of northern Italy. They're all written in an easy-to-follow, step-by-step style. This volume is also packed with useful information—for instance, a guide to using the different types of balsamic vinegars and tips on how to distinguish the sublime from the ordinary when buying Italian products.

CULTIVATED READING

Two new books help home growers make the most of their backyard bounty. *The Moosewood Restaurant Kitchen Garden* (Fireside, 1992) was written by David Hirsch, a longtime member of the well-known New York collective, Moosewood. It includes tips for the home farmer, advice on garden design and lots of guilt-free vegetarian recipes.

The Salad Lover's Garden (Doubleday, 1992) by Sam Bittman takes you from crop selection to soil preparation to harvest. It includes a summary of more than seventy varieties of lettuce and a list of suppliers for seeds and garden accessories.

🍎

COOKING WITH KIDS

Here's a cookbook that shows kids how to prepare tasty snacks that are not only good, but good for them. *Kitchen Fun for Kids* (Center for Science in the Public Interest, 1991) is by Michael Jacobson, Ph.D., and Laura Hill, R.D. Included are basic recipes for kid-pleasing, healthful snacks that are low in fat, cholesterol and sodium and high in fiber. The book's available for $14.95 from CSPI by calling 202-667-7483.

🍎

🍎 *Restaurants and People*

SOUTHERN STYLE

Want a taste of the real South? The Wild Boar Restaurant in Nashville serves a host of southern specialties, from starters like jumbo Gulf shrimp and Cajun crab cakes to such entrées as rabbit and speckled trout. But what's most "downhome" authentic is their Tennessee wild game sampler, which includes farmland quail, venison from the western part of the state and wild boar from the Great Smoky Mountains. (The Wild Boar Restaurant, 2014 Broadway, Nashville, TN 37203; 615-329-1313.)

🍎

NEW IN NEW ORLEANS

Susan Spicer, formerly of The Bistro at Maison de Ville, has opened her own place, Bayona, in a renovated Creole cottage with a garden courtyard. Her Mediterranean-inspired menu includes such specialties as roasted eggplant salad with *tapenade* (an anchovy-olive puree), fresh salmon with a white wine sauce and sauerkraut and *boudin noir* (blood sausage) with apples and onions. (Bayona, 430 Dauphine Street, New Orleans, LA 70112; telephone 504-525-4455.)

🍎

VIRGIN TERRITORY

The U.S. Virgin Islands offer some of the most creative restaurants in the Caribbean, especially St. Thomas. In Charlotte Amalie, energetic visitors can climb the 101 steps from the post office on Main Street up to The Mark St. Thomas. The reward? Original and superb food. Built in 1785, the graceful old mansion is constructed of pink ballast brick and stone, with lacy white wrought-iron verandas and balconies that overlook the glittering lights of the city's busy harbor. (The Mark St. Thomas, Blackbeard's Hill, Charlotte Amalie, St. Thomas, USVI 00802; 809-774-5511.)

CURRYING FAVOR IN LONDON

The Bombay Brasserie in South "Ken" is one of London's top curry houses. The clientele includes a good number of well-heeled Indian customers and, according to the menu, Faye Dunaway, who favors two of the restaurant's hotter curries. The menu covers the long sweep of the old Bombay Presidency, from fiery offerings of former Portuguese Goa in the south to dishes from the charcoal-fired tandoor clay oven, its origins on the chilly northwest frontier. (Bombay Brasserie, Courtfield Close, 140 Gloucester Road, South Kensington, London SW7; 071-370-4040.)

SCOTTSDALE PUB

At Hops! Bistro and Brewery, next to the Scottsdale Fashion Square, brewmaster Peter McFarlane makes pilsner, wheat beer, ale and seasonal draft beers to go with chef Joe DeLucia's healthful, something-for-everyone menu. Pastas, thin-crust pizzas, burgers and salads of locally grown greens are offered, along with such main courses as chicken with grilled vegetables, cheese polenta and tequila-lime sauce; grilled ahi tuna on young greens with teriyaki vinaigrette; and sliced spit-roasted leg of lamb with pan-roasted potatoes. (Hops! Bistro and Brewery, 7000 East Camelback Road, Scottsdale, AZ 85251; telephone 602-945-HOPS.)

🍎

HIGH DESIGN IN SANTA MONICA

Recently, the popular Röckenwagner relocated from Venice to Santa Monica, with new digs in the visually intriguing, Frank Gehry-designed Edgemar complex. Here, chef/owner Hans Röckenwagner turns out equally intriguing food, such as crab soufflé with lobster sauce; smoked chicken breast with a wild rice pancake and tamarind-

Champagne sauce; and warm apple "pizza," which combines puff pastry with almond cream and apples. (Röckenwagner, 2435 Main Street, Santa Monica, CA 90405; 310-399-6504.)

DOING DELI IN NEW YORK

If you like the idea of spotting a star or two while waiting for your pastrami on rye, head to midtown's Stage Deli, where the most unabashed celebrity watching takes place, as evidenced by the galaxy of Polaroids on the wall. The folks there even name sandwiches after them, such as the Dolly Parton: corned beef and pastrami on twin rolls, with coleslaw and Russian dressing. (Stage Deli, 834 Seventh Avenue, New York, NY 10019; 212-245-7850.)

LOS ANGELES: WATERFRONT DINING

Cafe Del Rey is a chic, airy restaurant that's not only right in the middle of the action along Marina del Rey's main channel, but also an excellent change of pace from the chain and hotel restaurants in the neighborhood. Executive chef Katsuo Nagasawa, formerly of La Petite Chaya, turns out a multi-ethnic menu combining Mediterranean, French, nouvelle California and Pacific Rim cuisines. Also, there's a Sunday brunch by the sea that's hard to beat. (Cafe Del Rey, 4451 Admiralty Way, Marina del Rey, CA 90292; telephone 310-823-6395.)

SEAFOOD BY THE LAKE IN SEATTLE

Puget Sound-area residents have long associated Russ Wohler with his immensely popular local eatery, Ray's Boathouse. Now they are also getting to know him for the Yarrow Bay Grill and Beach Café, a newer restaurant (actually two restaurants in one place) situated in Kirkland on the thriving eastern shore of Lake Washington. Downstairs at the come-as-you-are Beach Café, the food's casual and fun; upstairs at the Yarrow Bay Grill, the menu offers innovative dishes that use the best ingredients. (Yarrow Bay Grill and Beach Café, 1270 Carillon Point, Kirkland, WA 98033; 206-889-9052.)

HIP IN THE HAMPTONS

The biggest news of the 1992 summer season in New York's Hamptons was the revivial of the Dune Deck hotel's weathered dining room on Westhampton Beach. This was achieved at the hands of Starr Boggs, one of the most talented practitioners of fresh Long Island cuisine around. The cozy spot he used to occupy became Saffron, with chef-owner Ali Fathalla of Ca' Nova in Manhattan in charge. (Starr Boggs, 379 Dune Road, Westhampton Beach, NY 11978; 516-288-5250. Saffron, 23 Sunset Avenue, Westhampton Beach, NY 11978; 516-288-4610.)

ELEGANT SEAFOOD IN SAN FRANCISCO

George Morrone, a Bradley Ogden protégé and former chef at Los Angeles's Hotel Bel-Air, returned to San Francisco last year and opened the instantly popular Aqua. The idea behind this sleek and sophisticated place is all-seafood, "treated like a three-star restaurant would," says Morrone. Mahimahi with celery fumet and parsnip puree and tuna with foie gras and Pinot Noir sauce are two good examples. (Aqua, 252 California Street, San Francisco, CA 94111; 415-956-9662.)

WAIKIKI UPDATE

There's a new take on contemporary cuisine at Ciao Mein in the Hyatt Regency Waikiki in Honolulu. You can dine indoors or out at this sophisticated bistro-style restaurant, whose menu offers a variety of Italian and Chinese dishes with an eye to keeping things light, healthful and reasonably priced. (Ciao Mein, Hyatt Regency Waikiki, 2424 Kalakaua Avenue, Honolulu, HI 96815; 808-923-1234.)

🦢 *Getaways*

BIG SUR: BLISS ON A CLIFF

The Post Ranch Inn is the first luxury resort to be built in the Big Sur area in almost twenty years. There are thirty guest units on the secluded 98-acre site, including several sod-roofed "ocean houses" recessed into the side of the ridge, a two-story cylindrical structure plus a few spectacular stilted "treehouse" units. What they all share are privacy, interiors of wood and stone, large windows, verandas and views with a capital "V." (Post Ranch Inn, P.O. Box 219, Highway 1, Big Sur, CA 93920; 800-527-2200.)

🦢

ALBERTA MOUNTAIN SPOT

The Jasper Park Lodge, in Alberta's Jasper National Park, has long been a popular summertime playground; now it's a well-kept winter secret. The attractions are many: downhill and cross-country skiing, ice-skating, snowmobiling, sleigh rides and the like. Only 19 of the over four hundred rooms occupy the rambling, rustically elegant main lodge; others are scattered around the lake in log cabins and cedar chalets, many with fireplaces. And for meals, the Meadows Café serves casual fare all day, while the Edith Cavell Dining Room (named for the World War I English nursing hero) is the elegant evening place. (Jasper Park Lodge, P.O. Box 40, Jasper, Alberta T0E 1E0, Canada; 800-828-7447 or 403-852-3301.)

🦢

DELUXE ROCKIES SPA

The Doral Telluride Resort and Spa, set midmountain in the heart of the Telluride ski area, has more than terrific scenery: It has a four-level, 42,000-square-foot spa and athletic facility patterned after Doral's famous Saturnia International Spa Resort in Florida. There are many spa packages available, some pampering, some athletic, some both. There are two excellent restaurants, the Sundance and the Alpenglow, where executive chef Frank DeAmicis creates spa cuisine masterpieces. (Doral Telluride Resort and Spa, 136 Country Club Drive, Telluride, CO 81435; 800-22-DORAL.)

🦢

CANADA'S SALMON SPOT

From Vancouver or Seattle, a short, scenic flight in a float plane up the Strait of Georgia will land you in a great getaway vacation destination called April Point Lodge and Fishing Resort. Anglers come here hoping to catch giant Chinook salmon, but if fishing isn't what you had in mind, there's plenty more to do, including golf, tennis and horseback riding. Meals are delicious and generously portioned; accommodations come in the form of comfortable suites, guest houses, cabins and rooms. (April Point Lodge and Fishing Resort, P.O. Box 1, Campbell River, B.C., Canada V9W 4Z9; 604-285-2222.)

🦢

LUXURY IN SCOTTSDALE

In a town known for its mega-resorts, the new, 11-room Inn at the Citadel is a welcome change of pace. Nestled among the foothills of the Pinnacle Peak mountains at the north end of the city, the inn was built in the southwestern style, its interiors accented with antique as well as contemporary pieces. Verandas and fireplaces make in-room relaxation even cozier. Massages, facials and manicures are also available. In the morning, breakfast, coffee and a newspaper are delivered to your room. (The Inn at the Citadel; 8700 East Pinnacle Peak Road, Scottsdale, AZ 85255; 800-927-8367.)

OREGON: STORIED HOTEL

Sylvia Beach, an expatriate American who, in the twenties, owned a Paris bookstore that was a social center for the likes of Ernest Hemingway, T.S. Eliot and Gertrude Stein, is remembered at the Sylvia Beach Hotel in Newport, Oregon. Located above peaceful Nye Beach, about a hundred miles southwest of Portland, the inn has twenty rooms named after famous writers and decorated appropriately with antiques and images from well-known works. It's a great place for book lovers who want to read, relax and talk, away from radios, phones and television. At mealtime, the conviviality continues at the Tables of Content restaurant. (Sylvia Beach Hotel, 267 Northwest Cliff Street, Newport, OR 97365; 503-265-5428.)

SAN FRANCISCO: NEW HOTEL BY THE BAY

San Francisco hotelier Bill Kimpton has opened yet another "small" hotel to add to his group, which includes the Villa Florence, Harbor Court Hotel and the Hotel Vintage Court. His newest venture, the avant-garde Hotel Triton, is located in the heart of the gallery district. Here, Louis XIV meets art deco and art nouveau, in rooms and suites decorated with eclectic verve and enhanced by such unusual touches as yellow-and-blue harlequin-patterned walls that were painted by local artists. The hotel adjoins two new restaurants: Aïoli serves a Mediterranean mix of pastas, salads, sandwiches and light meals; Cafe de la Presse is a European-style coffeehouse with a newsstand. (Hotel Triton, 342 Grant Avenue, San Francisco, CA 94108; 800-433-6611.)

SPAIN: ELITE RETREAT

Where do Barcelona's elite go when they want to get away from it all? Many of them head for the Hotel Mas de Torrent, an elegantly restored eighteenth-century farmhouse in the hills above the bustling Costa Brava. An intimate size (just thirty guest rooms), private gardens and sophisticated country dining are just some of the lures. The spectacular scenery is another. (Hotel Mas de Torrent, 17123 Torrent, Gerona, Spain; telephone number (72) 30.32.92.)

SAN DIEGO ELEGANT

Completed in 1970, the Westgate is an extravagant, stylish hotel in the middle of what is perhaps the ultimate California beach town—San Diego. The lobby was designed as a recreation of one of the anterooms of the Palace of Versailles; the concierge desk also has a twin at Versailles. The dramatic decor continues throughout the 223 guest rooms, where antiques and artwork combine with Italian marble bathrooms with brass appointments for a truly opulent feeling. At the hotel's Le Fontainebleau restaurant, executive chef William Henley prepares food with traditional French touches. (The Westgate Hotel and Le Fontainebleau, 1055 Second Avenue, San Diego, CA 92101; 619-238-1818.)

WYOMING: OLD WEST RANCH

Cody's Ranch Resort, owned by the wife of "Buffalo Bill" Cody's grandson, is located in a secluded mountain valley just east of Yellowstone National Park in the Shoshone National Forest. Pine, aspen and cottonwood trees surround the fourteen deluxe cabins, and thousands of acres of adjacent Wyoming wilderness provide an appropriate backdrop. A variety of horseback rides takes visitors of all abilities into the high country; and, back in the main lodge, hearty dinners might include brook trout, chili or rib-eye steak. (Cody's Ranch Resort, 2604 Yellowstone Highway, Cody, WY 82414; telephone 307-587-6271.)

🍒 *For the Kitchen and Table*

ROYAL TREATMENT

To create her truly unique plates and platters, designer Susan Ward first paints an original composition, then affixes it to the underside of a clear plate and seals it with layers of lacquer. The limited-edition designs range from the ornate and vibrant "Royal Family" to a romantic, pastel-colored rendering called "Peaches and Grapes." Prices run from about $90 for an 8-inch plate to $200 for a 13-inch platter. For more information, call 212-334-0064 or 212-627-1263.

🍒

TABLE GUARD

Protect the dining table from hot serving dishes with a stylish trivet from Virginia Metalcrafters. Handmade of cast iron and fashioned after a traditional symbol of hospitality, the "Newport Pineapple" design is $25. Call 703-949-9400 for a store near you.

🍒

PORTABLE GARDEN

The rustic "Green Thumb" planter's box makes a marvelous centerpiece when filled with pots of herbs or flowers. Constructed of rough-hewn wood, it's just the size for holding two rows of small pots (it measures 12x23x15 inches). From Garden Source Furnishings in Atlanta, the box costs about $40 (there's also a smaller, 7-inch-wide version for $32). For locations, call 404-351-6446.

🍒

PLATE ON THE WING

Noted Limoges designer André Raynaud was so taken by the Carven Collection of oriental porcelain birds in the Guimet Museum in Paris that he fashioned the feathered "Ramage" dinnerware pattern. Each five-piece place setting is about $350 at Neiman-Marcus stores across the country.

🍒

FINISHING TOUCH

Sarah Frederick uses an unusual technique to create a lovely matte finish on her melon teapot and tea bowls. The Louisville potter airbrushes the glaze onto the stoneware before firing; the resulting surface really does resemble that of a melon. Her work is represented by the Kentucky Art and Craft Gallery in Louisville, which also produces Made in Kentucky, a catalog featuring other Kentucky crafts. The teapot is $300; the tea bowls are $30 each. To order or to request a catalog, call 502-589-0102 or 800-446-0102.

🍒

FRENCH BUFFET

The Pierre Picard line of hand-forged iron furniture from France strikes the perfect balance between earthy and elegant. One of our favorite pieces is the glass-topped "Marlena" console. With hammered, hand-polished iron detailing and lustrous finish, the console makes an exquisite buffet or sideboard. For details, call Ironware International in Nashville; 615-269-5657.

🍒

MAG-NEATO

Liven up refrigerator messages with charming fruit and vegetable magnets from Accessories, Etc. Made of durable resin and painted by hand, the 2- to 3-inch-tall pieces (there are 25 kinds in all) cost about $4 each. Find a bumper crop at specialty shops and department stores across the country; call 800-782-3493 or 813-951-2066 for store locations.

🍒

STRIKING IRON

Virginia craftsman Peter O'Shaughnessy uses traditional blacksmithing techniques to forge iron into shapes of amazing delicacy—like his splendid serpentine candle holder. It costs $136; order by calling 703-261-2010.

DIAMONDS ARE . . .

. . . a chef's best friend. That is, if you're talking about the amazing new diamond-grit sharpening steels from The Ultimate Edge. The lightweight, oval-shaped sharpeners come in five sizes, cost $13.50 to $36 and are available in specialty stores nationwide. For more information or to order, telephone 310-828-3989.

SHARP AND SLEEK

The LamsonSharp Chinese Knife from Lamson & Goodnow is a real find. It's well balanced and sturdy, with a sharp yet surprisingly thin edge that makes it useful for tough jobs as well as more delicate tasks. The 10-inch steel and rosewood knife costs about $40 at kitchen shops nationwide; telephone 413-625-6331 for locations.

A NEW ANGLE

Revere's "Spectrum" cookware features double pour spouts and a cover with holes on both sides that allow for easy straining—and for steam to escape. The new aluminum cookware also has a nonstick interior and an easy-to-clean enamel finish in three jewel-tone metallic colors. A seven-piece set is about $120 in department stores nationwide.

SALAD DAYS

Reed & Barton's salad servers made of silver plate and French olive wood can accent both formal and casual tables beautifully. The set, called "Corinthian" ($89, plus shipping), makes a terrific wedding gift or special present for a hostess. To order, call The Fantastic Catalog Company at 800-527-6566.

GARDEN OF EATIN'

The new vegetable-patterned earthenware "Cannella" plates from Cherubini set a cheerful table. Hand-painted in Italy, the dessert-size plates are $35 each; dinner plates and serving pieces are also available. For stores, call 212-768-0646.

CLEAR CHEER

Translucent tinted Martini glasses from Mila International will add a shimmery glow to any celebration. Part of the "Rainbow Glass" collection, the 6-ounce design costs about $18 and comes in a variety of color combinations, such as violet and green. There are several shapes available, too. For store locations, call 800-275-1952 or 404-352-2664.

AMERICAN BEAUTY

"American Garden," the newest porcelain pattern from Tiffany & Co., adds a fresh, flowery touch to the table. The design was inspired by plants native to the United States—from Indian corn to Texas bluebonnets. To order the five-piece place settings ($325 each), call Tiffany & Co. at 800-526-0649 or 212-755-8000.

SUPER GLASS

For serving poolside or outdoor drinks, our vote goes to the new unbreakable stemware from Möller International Design. Fashioned from the same space-age plastic used for the F-14 cockpit domes, the glasses won't crack or discolor like those made of acrylic or other plastic and are microwave- and dishwasher-safe. Available in several colors, the 8-ounce flutes and goblets, as well as tumblers, are $5 to $7 each. Call 800-866-5537 for store locations.

LOBSTER TALES

Whether the menu calls for elegant seafood mousse or fresh steamed crabs piled high on a platter, Liz Wain's hand-painted linen "Lobster" napkins will complement any "fishy" place setting. Find the 20x20-inch napkins at Events gift shop in Houston for $41.95 each, plus shipping. To order, telephone 800-662-5199.

❦ *Diet News*

SLIMMING DOWN SOUTH

The heart of historic Charleston is the backdrop for a new fitness package offered by The Omni Hotel at Charleston Place. The two-week Charleston Retreat program combines lodging and healthful meals at the posh Omni, with individual counseling on weight management at the nearby Medical University of South Carolina (MUSC). The program also includes a physical examination and customized diet and exercise plans. Leisure time can be spent taking in Antique Row, art galleries, museums and the antebellum homes along The Battery. For more information, call MUSC's Weight Management Center at 800-553-7489 or 803-792-2273.

❦

GAME WINNER

On the lookout for a new low-fat protein source? Well, what about rabbit? This naturally lean meat is high in protein, iron and vitamin B_{12} and low in the big four: fat, cholesterol, calories and sodium. And rabbit's mild flavor is perfect for everything from stir-frying to roasting to barbecuing. Many specialty meat markets carry rabbit, and at least one purveyor, Classic Country Rabbit Company in Oregon, ships its product direct. For a free mail-order brochure and price list, telephone 800-821-7426.

❦

CHEERS FOR KIWI

California kiwi fruit, which comes into season in the fall, is packed with nutritional value. Ounce for ounce, it has as much potassium as bananas, twice the vitamin C of oranges, three times that of grapefruit, and lots of dietary fiber. Each refreshing emerald-green fruit comes with only about 45 calories, and to top all that good news, the fuzzy brown skin is edible—although we suspect that it might be something of an acquired taste.

THE GRAINING OF AMERICA

A lot of people don't know beans when it comes to grains, says a new Gallup poll conducted for the Wheat Foods Council. Nearly half of those in the survey did not know that white bread is made from wheat, and the same number incorrectly identified oatmeal as wheat. Disturbing news, in light of the heavy emphasis the USDA's new Food Guide Pyramid gives to the grains group, which includes bread, cereal, rice and pasta.

Many respondents also associated grains with fattening calories, when, in fact, grains are extremely low in calories and fat. And, as an abundant source of energizing complex carbohydrates, the calories from grains are among the most useful we can get.

For more information or to order their brochures, *Facts About Fiber* and *Facts About Carbohydrates*, send a business-size S.A.S.E. to the Wheat Foods Council, 5500 South Quebec, No. 111, Englewood, CO 80111.

❦

BREW THE RIGHT THING

The nineties are the time to make environmentally sound and socially responsible choices, right down to the morning cup of joe. The Thanksgiving Coffee Company supplies organic coffees and chemical-free decaffeinated varieties, plowing some of the profits back into environmental, educational and athletic programs. For a free catalog, call 800-648-6491 or 707-964-0118.

THIS BIRD IS CURED

Love beef jerky but concerned that it has too much fat and sodium? Consider turkey instead. Top of the Flock Turkey Jerky has plenty of flavor, but less than a gram of fat per 1-ounce snack pack. In addition, it has much less salt than most beef jerky (499 milligrams per ounce compared to beef's 800 milligrams) and no preservatives. It's available by mail order. Telephone 818-246-5556 (in California) or 700-246-5556.

ORGANIC TOMATOES

Tomatoes true to nature. That's what Muir Glen Organic Tomato Products promises—and delivers. Their deep-red tomatoes, organically grown and processed in California, are free of synthetic pesticides, fertilizers and growth regulators. Further, their product line of tomatoes, sauces, puree and tomato paste is packed in lead-free, enamel-lined recyclable cans with labels printed on recycled paper. Want more? The company also donates 10 percent of its profits to environmental programs. Available in natural foods stores across the country.

LOW-FAT CAKES

If it's a cake and it arrives in the mail, it must be a fruitcake, right? Not! It could be the new cholesterol-free low-fat loaf cakes from Harry and David in Medford, Oregon. These light and moist cakes, with only a single gram of fat per 2-ounce serving, come in chocolate, apple spice with streusel, and lemon. The three arrive packaged together for $17.95. To order or for a catalog featuring fresh fruits and other natural goodies, call 800-547-3033.

LOBSTER FACTS

The folks at the Maine Lobster Promotion Council think their favorite crustacean has been getting a bad rap on fat, and they're out to set the record straight. First of all, lobster is named in a National Institutes of Health report as a food lower in fats, calories and cholesterol than skinless white-meat chicken—and that's pretty low. Second, it contains beneficial omega-3 fish oils, which are thought to lower cholesterol levels. It seems lobster has been guilty only by association: The real culprit is the melted butter that's usually served with it.

QUICK CHICKEN

A new breed of take-out restaurants is finding big success with healthful chicken-to-go. The specialty at Boston Chicken, a Chicago-based chain of prepared-food stores now opening nationwide, is marinated, slow-roasted chicken—a better bet than fried—with dietwise dishes on the side. For locations, call 708-955-6100. Even lower in fat and cholesterol is the chicken at Koo Koo Roo, a Los Angeles-based fast-food chain also headed for the national market. Their skinless, flame-broiled chicken is marinated in vegetable juices and spices, and has far less fat than most fried and rotisserie-cooked chicken. For locations near you, call 310-479-2080.

EATING FOR TWO

Proper eating habits are especially important for expectant mothers. That's why the March of Dimes Birth Defects Foundation and the International

Food Information Council have put together *Healthy Eating During Pregnancy*, a 16-page booklet full of practical, up-to-date information on maternity nutrition. For a free copy, send a self-addressed mailing label to *Healthy Eating During Pregnancy*, P.O. Box 1144, Rockville, MD 20850. Also available from the March of Dimes is Eating for Two, a packet of healthful recipes. It's distributed from local chapters of the organization.

❦

A VOTE FOR BROCCOLI

Broccoli keeps rising in its star status among vegetables. We knew it had beta carotene, but now Dr. Paul Talalay of the Johns Hopkins University School of Medicine has found that broccoli also contains sulforaphane, a powerful natural chemical that helps protect against cancer. But broccoli is not alone: The American Cancer Society expects more studies to reveal the cancer-preventive qualities of other fruits and vegetables, and health officials continue to recommend that Americans increase their consumption of fruits and vegetables to at least five servings a day.

❦

🍒 Credits and Acknowledgments

The following people and restaurants contributed the recipes included in this book:

1701 Cafe, The Warwick, Philadelphia,
  Pennsylvania
Arnie's and Morton's of Chicago, Chicago,
  Illinois
Au Pied de Cochon, Paris, France
Leah Balk
Melanie Barnard
Patricia and Rick Barrow
The Blue Lion Restaurant, Jackson Hole,
  Wyoming
The Boulders, Carefree, Arizona
Bovine Bakery, Pt. Reyes Station, California
Deborah Briggs
Sabine Broeck-Sallah
Ann M. Brown
Cafe Zelo, Corvallis, Oregon
California Cafe Bar & Grill, Yountville,
  California
Campanile Restaurant, Los Angeles,
  California
C'est la Vie, Anchorage, Alaska
Chasen's, West Hollywood, California
Michael Chiabaudo
The Chipman Inn, Ripton, Vermont
Debra and James Cianciolo
Ciro's Cibi Italiani, Houston, Texas
Harry Colcord
Patti and David Cottle
Lane S. Crowther
Kathi Dameron
Deli de Pasta, Yakima, Washington
Brooke Dojny
Falcon Lodge, Bangor, Maine
Gary N. Fauskin
Mark Flemming
Brad Fox

Ruth Gardner-Loew
Gelson's Market, Encino, California
Grand Hyatt Wailea Resort & Spa, Maui,
  Hawaii
Green's at Fort Wayne, San Francisco,
  California
Theresa Hansen
Jessica Elin Hirschman
The Home Ranch, Clark, Colorado
Huggery Restaurant, Deer Valley Resort,
  Park City, Utah
Il Fiorentino, Kenmore, New York
Karen A. Kaplan
Jeanne Thiel Kelley
Kelly's on Trinity, San Francisco, California
Kristine Kidd
Theresa Korchynsky
La Cremaillere Restaurant, San Francisco,
  California
La Cuineta, Barcelona, Spain
La Marmotte Restaurant, Telluride, Colorado
Le Manoir aux Quat' Saisons, Oxford,
  England
Le Petit Marguery, Paris, France
Julie R. Littlejohn-Dunlap
Mauna Lani Bay Hotel & Bungalows,
  Kohala Coast, Hawaii
Memory and Company Restaurant,
  Charlottesville, Virginia
Michael McLaughlin
Marie T. Mora
Selma Brown Morrow
Murphin Ridge Inn, West Union, Ohio
Ojai Valley Inn & Country Club, Ojai,
  California
Parador Gil Blas, Santillana.del Mar, Spain

Mary Anne Penton
Rathsallagh House, Dunn Lavin, Ireland
Ritz-Carlton Chicago, Chicago, Illinois
Marilou Robinson
Carol Rock
The Rowe, Ellsworth, Michigan
RoxSand, Phoenix, Arizona
Richard Sax
Debbie and William Schwartz
Scottish Lion Inn, North Conway Village,
  New Hampshire
Mary Sellen
Edena Sheldon
Marie Simmons
Kay Sisk
Sharon Smith
Gil Martinez Soto
Spoons Grill & Bar, Newport Beach,
  California
Steve Sunyog
Christine Swanson
Tapawingo, Ellsworth, Michigan
Sarah Tenaglia
Thai Pepper, Ashland, Oregon
Susan Tollefson
Topnotch at Stowe Resort and Spa, Stowe,
  Vermont
Tutti's, Montecito, California
The Underground Deli, Ashland, Oregon
Uptown Cafe, Butte, Montana
Vincent Guerithault on Camelback,
  Phoenix, Arizona
Glenn Weber
Jason Williams
Jennifer Lind Yarlott
Desiree Zamorano

"News '92" text supplied by James Badham, Sarah Belk and Vené Franco

Foreword and chapter introductions written by Laurie Glenn Buckle

Editorial Staff:
  William J. Garry
  Barbara Fairchild
  Laurie Glenn Buckle

Copy Editor:
  Marilyn Novell

Rights and Permissions:
  Gaylen Ducker Grody

Graphics Staff:
  Bernard Rotondo
  Sandy Douglas

Production:
  Joan Valentine

Indexer:
  Barbara Wurf

The Knapp Press
is a wholly owned subsidiary of
KNAPP COMMUNICATIONS CORPORATION

Composition by Andresen Graphic Services, Tucson, Arizona

This book is set in Sabon, a face designed by Jan Teischold in 1967
and based on early fonts engraved by Garamond and Granjon.